My Parents are Divorced, too

My Parents are Divorced, too

Teenagers Talk
About Their Experiences
And How They Cope

Bonnie Robson, M.D.

EVEREST HOUSE
New York

**Library of Congress Cataloging
in Publication Data**

Robson, Bonnie, 1940–
  My parents are divorced, too.

SUMMARY: Interviews with 28 young people explore
their understanding of their parents' divorce, what
caused it, their feelings about it, and how they coped
with it.

  1. Children of divorced parents—Canada.
  2. Divorce—Canada. 3. Adolescent psychology.
  [1. Divorce] I. Title.
HQ755.5.C2R62 1980   306.8'9   79-91417

ISBN 0-89696-091-9

Contents

Acknowledgements

This book was written by the adolescents who participated in the project. Without their willingness to share their own experiences with others it could not have been undertaken. I have a great deal of admiration for this fine group of people. I have attempted to bring together their thoughts and feelings so that other adolescents in similar circumstances may gain understanding and comfort.

Throughout the project, from its inception until today, many people have contributed through suggestion, assistance and encouragement. I am glad to be able to express my appreciation to all of them.

As the director of a psychiatric service, Dr. A.M. Hood has always encouraged his staff to undertake projects of special interest and has offered whatever resources he can to promote work of a preventative nature. This project could not have been completed without his wholehearted support. His approval and encouragement have meant much more than he will ever willingly acknowledge.

I wish to express my appreciation to Dr. Q. Rae-Grant and Dr. P. Steinhauer, Professors of Child Psychiatry at the University of Toronto, for their encouragement and suggestions in the early stages.

I am indebted to Dr. B. Killinger for her insistence that even clinicians need a methodology. She helped in the preparation of the two questionnaires and participated in the interviewing. Her warmth and quiet manner were much appreciated by the adolescents who met with her. One of the worst tasks in a project like this is the tedious hours spent transcribing, by hand, the prerecorded tapes. Evan Collins, Mali McIntosh and Robert Feher attacked this aspect of the project with enthusiasm.

Background research for this project would not have been accomplished without the assistance of Mrs. Betty Mair, the librarian at the C.M. Hincks Treatment Centre. Betty is ever alert to the needs of numerous people, and her resourcefulness in finding out-of-print texts and unusual articles is phenomenal. Mrs. A. Wilson handled the administrative and financial aspects of the project with her usual calm efficiency. I very much appreciate her willingness to add yet another project to her already overburdened schedule.

My secretary, Nora Such, was untiring in her labor. She typed the transcripts of the first interviews weekend after weekend. She struggled with my own scrawl, directions and counterdirections with, if not enthusiasm, a dedication and devotion for which I am deeply grateful.

Larry Goldstein came around to my office for an hour one day last fall. He stayed for five. He said that this project must be completed. He pushed and prodded and he believed in it.

Toronto,
October 2nd, 1978

My Parents
are Divorced, too

1
What's This All About?

I am a child psychiatrist. I talk with people who have problems with school, with their families or with friends. When one person in a family — whether a child, an adolescent or a parent — comes to see me, I usually like to talk with everybody in the family, because if one person is having problems it affects everyone around him or her. If there is a problem in the family, like a recent separation or divorce, it affects everyone in the family.

Three years ago now, I met with several families for the first time just as they were thinking of a separation. I was surprised that of all the people in the family, children and parents, the adolescent members seemed most able to understand what was happening and most able to deal with the problems that automatically come with a separation. The adolescents did not particularly want to talk with me about any difficulties at the time. I said, "Fine, but if anything comes up that you want to talk about, get in touch with me." I was surprised when about a year later I heard from these teenagers, all of whom had questions or ideas they wanted to sound out with me. These teenagers didn't have deep psychological problems but they did have very valid concerns arising from the separation of their parents. As we talked I realized I had *some* of the answers — but not all of them. I asked my colleagues, "What normally happens to a teenager whose parents divorce?" It may surprise you that my colleagues were also wondering the same thing. Everyone seems to be aware of the problem of divorce today, but not many people have answers to the questions. I wasn't even sure if we had all the questions. The solution to this situation is obvious: ask the people who know most about it, the people who, during their teen years, have lived through their parents' separation and divorce. And that's what I did.

This book is the result of many hours of conversation and exchange of ideas with adolescents who know firsthand about divorce. I want to share their experience, their knowledge, their mistakes, their gains and their advice with you, because I believe that real understanding and empathy come through experience. Also, I think that an "expert" always sounds like a lecturer and while his or her advice may be sound it seems much easier, at times, to hear it from a peer who shares the same experiences.

Who are these adolescents who are willing to share their thoughts and experiences? The 28 people in the group are between 11 and 18 years of age. Their parents' separations all happened more than a year ago and for some as many as five years ago. The people who talked with me are not people who came to see me because of their problems. They are all volunteers who wanted to share their feelings and opinions with other people. Some of them said they came to be part of the project because they wished that someone had told them what would happen when their parents first divorced. So if you are an adolescent whose parents are separating, this book is for you. In a way it's a gift from the people in the project. It wasn't always easy for them to relive their past by talking about it, but they did so in the hope that they might lessen the pain and hurt of others.

Bill, who is 11, is the youngest person in the group. His parents separated just one year ago. He remembers being wakened in the night by arguments since he was about nine and feels his parents separated because they just couldn't get along. His dad moved out but not far away. Bill, his brother and mother stayed on in the house. In some ways things are much better for Bill now. He sees a lot more of his father: "Because before Dad got home late from work. In the morning he was in bed. Saturdays he had to work. Now he takes me with him to work."

Karen, who is 12, is the only person whose parents have joint custody. She and her younger sister live six months with their mother and six months with their father. Their parents live close together so the girls can stay at the same school. It's been a year and a half since Karen's parents separated because they had totally different values and lifestyles. The whole family has become more active since the separation. Karen is involved in horseback riding, gymnastics and skiing.

Sharon, age 12, has a sister six years older than her. Even without her sister's help Sharon was able to figure out that her father was not sleeping at the factory but had his own apartment. The family has had a lot of problems with finances and Sharon and her sister got caught in the middle. Her sister and her mother argue a lot and Sharon is afraid her sister will get kicked out: "I don't want my sister to go because my sister and I are very close. She does two jobs and she's earning a lot of money." Sharon sometimes worries about her mother, who has become very bitter about money.

Dawn is 12. She has an older sister and a younger brother. Her parents separated slightly over a year ago: "My father was an alcoholic and my mother hated it when he came home late at night drunk." They had to move to a smaller house just recently because of the high rent in their old home. Dawn thinks it's important that kids stay together. She likes the new house. It's very open and she has lots more friends who just walk in.

Nancy, 13, and her young sister were quite shocked by their father's announcement that he was moving to an apartment. At first they really resented his girlfriend, but now they like her. But he's had to move away now to find a job. The girls and their mother had to move as well: "We had to get rid of the dog and everything. I used to say it's all his fault. My mom cried a lot, not every day, but a lot. She has to work now and when she gets home she just puts the stereo earphones on and lies on her bed. She doesn't do the dishes, the laundry, anything. She's just zonked."

Annette, age 14, has an older and a younger brother. Her father has remarried. Annette found that her closest friend was of real help to her at first: "She just talked to me for hours and just comforted me, and it made me feel better." Annette lives with her mother.

She is angry at her father's wife: "She was married before and she has a child from her previous marriage and it's really hard to see her with my father. We still see my father and talk to him and everything. We don't dislike him because of what happened."

Bev is 14 and has a younger brother and sister. They are living with their mother. "My dad was an alcoholic and he never used to pay the bills and my mum got fed up so they separated." Bev worries that her father is lonely and that he doesn't have a job. She wishes the final decision had not been so sudden.

Jim, age 15, and his second oldest brother live with their father. They have some difficulties — three men managing a house. Both Jim's mother and father remarried, and now his father has separated again with a second divorce pending. So Jim has five step-brothers and sisters. His oldest brother is living on his own. Jim feels he's much more responsible because of the separation. He works in a restaurant about 5 hours a week.

Sally, 15, has an older sister, and they live with their mother. For two years after the separation they lived with a friend of their mother's and his two children. Although Sally felt this friend helped and understood about divorce, she didn't like his taking charge. Sally feels it will be hard for her, as the youngest, to leave home because then her mother will be alone. Sally has joined drama classes and participates in a lot of sports as well as doing a lot more work around the house.

Joel is 15. He's the youngest in the family with an older brother and sister. Just he and his sister live with their mother — his older brother has gone away to study. Joel is the only one in the family who tries to see his father regularly: "My father went to live with his parents and I began visiting him regularly on the weekends and we would always have a very good time. My sister never goes."

Abby, 16, has a younger sister. Her parents separated when she was 11 and divorced when she was 15. Her father has since remarried. Although she's grown closer to her mother, with whom she lives, she visits with her father Thursday nights for dinner and sometimes Saturdays if she doesn't have too much homework. At first, Abby didn't tell many of her friends that her parents were separated: "I was embarrassed about it and it was kind of awkward because not many people's parents were divorced, but now I'm pretty open about it because a lot of my friends' parents have gone through the same thing."

Barry, who is 16, lives with his mother and two older sisters. It's been three years now since his parents separated. He works at odd jobs and as a summer camp counsellor. He is interested in fishing, art and painting and is very active in sports, such as cross-country running and team swimming. Barry says he learned from the separation that his parents are just people who sometimes make mistakes. "I think another positive thing came out of the separation. I've never been close to my sisters. I loved them, of course, but I was never close. After that I was just so close to my mother and my sisters. I guess you have to be to survive."

Jill, 16, is an only child. She and her mother have remained in the same home since her father left two years ago. Jill's father is actually her step-father: "He married my mother when I was so young that it's just as though he's my father. I don't remember having another father. We were really poor but when they married we started a whole new life. He rescued us. It was lovely and then there were so many tensions. Now that he's gone the house is very relaxed and the greatest thing is I get along with him much better now. A lot of my friends really envy the way we get along now. And I'm really thankful for it."

Richard is 16. His parents separated when he was 13 and divorced when he was 15. Richard has an older and a younger brother. All three of them live with their mother. Richard's father lost his job because of the separation. This meant great financial difficulties for the family. His mother was quite depressed and very worried for some time, and she still often sits at home and does nothing. He tries to help her as best he can: as well as going to school, he works regularly and misses "a sense of family life."

John, 16, lives with his mother and younger sister. At first, John wanted to live with his father, but his parents decided that he should stay with his mother. Now he thinks that this was the right thing to do. At first, visiting his father on weekends was difficult: "We would go up there and play football and I'd drop the ball and it was a mortal sin. I was a 'fool', an 'idiot': 'You take after your mother.' Now he doesn't do it as much. It worked out to be better afterwards. Things were tense before they split up. Now I see how much better it is."

Duncan is 16 and lives with his father and twenty-three-year-old brother. His mother remarried when he was 14, but he still sees her every weekend: "She comes over when she wants and I guess they're glad to see each other. They talk a lot and sit in the living room." Duncan feels that he and his mother are good friends and that with his father it's just as if nothing happened. Duncan is active in tennis and football.

Jeff is 17 and lives on his own now. He was 14 when he came to the city with his mother, leaving an older sister and younger brother at home with his father. Jeff thinks this was one of the hardest decisions he ever made because, "we were always close. We would always stick together as a group. I have found out that not all divorces were as bad as my parents'. But basically everyone has the same feelings about it." Jeff is in his last year of high school and getting help through a government grant to complete his schooling. He left home because "Mother was never home and I had to do all the cleaning. It's a good arrangement because I live right around the corner."

Barbara is 17. She has four older brothers but just her next oldest brother and she are at home with their mother. Her father is an alcoholic and her mother got a divorce after a psychologist explained to her that there was "no chance of Father stopping drinking." Barbara had trouble accepting her mother's boyfriend: "I realize now I shouldn't deny her loving another man. I am not selfish. I'm worried what will happen to her when I leave. Mom's Catholic and she's always saying she doesn't think she could ever live with a person because it would be completely against her religion."

Harold, 17, has lived for periods of time with both his

mother and his father, as have his older brother and sister. Harold feels he made mistakes: "Don't try to get yourself kicked out because you don't have to try very hard: it will happen." Harold feels that his parents should never have sold their house, as it was a home base for all the children. Harold thinks his mother really understands all he went through. He feels he is now more independent than he might have been. Harold is a pretty good musician, plays baseball and soccer and enjoys water skiing.

Elizabeth is 17. She lives with her mother and younger sister. She thinks the reason her parents separated was that "my mother couldn't live with my father any more. He was quick-tempered and used to physically lash out to show his emotions. He couldn't speak them. Not trusting my mother was what my father's problem was. They're apart now and enjoying their own lives. My mother loves the feel of freedom and it's finally calming down. Ever since the separation we have lived in one house. My mother wanted my sister and I to have a stable secure place to call home."

Marion, 18, lives with her mother in the family home. Her older sister no longer lives at home. Her parents separated just over a year ago and got a divorce this year. Her father has remarried: "There's just the two of us in the house so we talk more and pay more attention to each other. We have a friendship." Marion is involved in church activities, choir and sports. She works as a swimming instructor and does well at school.

Margaret is 18. She feels her parents' separation last year has really helped her to mature. She moved to a school where she has more options, and she feels more able to make her own decisions now. Her older brother is away studying and she lives with her mother and younger brother. Gymnastic competitions and skiing occupy much of Margaret's free time. She feels very responsible for her mother's happiness and tries not to leave her alone.

Ted, 18, lives with his mother and younger sister. He gives his father's problem with alcohol as the reason for his parents' divorce two years ago. Ted is active in hockey, football and politics. He sees his father once or twice a month, "if I'm lucky." "I'm glad in a sense that I went through that experience. I could see myself becoming an alcoholic in a sense if I were to hang around with certain people. I've gotten to the point where I can control myself mainly because of what I've seen of my father. I worry that he is mentally and physically deteriorating."

Laurie, 18, is living with her boyfriend and her younger brother. Her parents separated when she was 14 and her father remarried last year. Right after the separation Laurie wanted to run away, but now she feels that, even though it was hard to stay home and work it through, she left feeling much closer and warmer towards her mother than she would have. Laurie wanted to be part of the project because, "I thought if I could help anyone going through separation and divorce it would be worth it."

Bob, 18, has a younger brother and sister. When his parents separated he was 15 and Bob got a job as a dishwasher: "It was the worst job I've ever had in my life, but it helped me. When I got back at the end of the summer everything was settling down. All the pain was sort of drained away by that time." Bob will finish high school this year and plans to go away to university next year. He is a volunteer television broadcaster in his spare time.

Jerry, 18, was just 12 when his parents first separated. He lives with his father and two brothers: an older brother lives away from home. Jerry feels that both his parents helped him by talking with him about the separation and giving him advice. He works twenty-four hours a week during school and fifty hours a week in the summer. He gives his father some money, buys groceries for the family sometimes and pays for all his own activities, such as tennis. He likes fishing and camping.

Michael is 18. Two older sisters are no longer living at home, but five years ago they were very comforting and talked to him when he was confused about the separation. Michael lives with his mother and plans to move out after he finishes university. Although he feels his mother is "more emotionally stable" since the divorce, he worries about what will happen to her when she is alone: "It's easier when parents are married or have someone. You feel they'll be all right. When all the kids are gone they'll really be alone, and when they get old who will care for them?" Michael has an interest in photography.

Gordon, 18, is living on his own and finds it hard because he's lonely and doesn't know how to cook very well yet. After his mother moved away, Gordon lived with his father and just moved out recently. While still in school, he works, is a member of a chess club, plays rugby and badminton and enjoys writing.

The next chapters follow this group from their initial awareness when faced with divorce or separation to their final conclusions about the subject. Included, in their own words, are their experiences and their advice for others. I don't agree with some of the advice that is offered, but I have neither excluded nor edited any remarks on that basis. Occasionally I take the liberty of pointing out an alternate plan of action. But basically this book is directed at responsible individuals whom I expect to weigh any advice very carefully before acting. You must accept the responsibility to filter out those suggestions that do not fit for you.

I find it helpful to remember that each individual's experience is unique. What applies to one person may be disastrous for another. At times of great stress, people tend to overreact, and in situations where I think this happened I have tried to explain what I think may have occurred and why.

Sometimes I refer to teenagers or adolescents as children. I have done this when I want to emphasize the child role in a parent-child relationship. It may help to remember that someone who is 65 has parents, even though they may be deceased. I can assure you of the respect I have for the maturity of the group, many of whom I found to be very responsible and farsighted compared with many people of the same age.

Let me add just one more note of caution before you begin. It may seem, at times, that in order to clarify certain feelings or thoughts of some of the adolescents I have overemphasized a certain perspective. If you don't share a particular feeling or find it to be true in your experience, this doesn't mean that your reaction is unusual or strange, but rather that it's one which just hasn't been emphasized. If you do have additional thoughts, opinions, or experiences that are not given sufficient weight, I'd like to hear from you: you can write to me care of the publisher's address. I would ask only that you seek your parents' opinion about writing me before doing so. My colleagues and I — as well as other adolescents — do need to know more about the adolescent's experience in parental separation or divorce.

2
It Hit Me Like a Brick Wall.

When your parents tell you they are going to live apart it's a shock — even if you've been expecting it to happen. Your interest in this book probably means that your parents have already separated or indicated by the way they've been talking to one another that a separation is imminent. So, you may be familiar with the feelings that occur just prior to the announcement and immediately after. Some of the people I talked to had a strong feeling that this experience had never happened to anyone else. You probably know what it's like to look out the window and see other people going about their business, and wonder why the world hasn't stopped for everyone as it has for you. The knowledge that right this minute someone else is going through the same thing can sometimes make you feel less alone.

Barbara recalls this sense of isolation: "At first they didn't say anything about a divorce. My father just went off. There was nothing final like, dad was just going on a trip. I didn't think of it that my dad was never coming back. Then it sort of dawned on me.

When it first happened to me it seemed like I was all alone, like as if there was no one else in the world that ever had a divorce. Later on I heard there were other people in the same position. But at the time I thought I was the only one."

Abby also felt alone and confused. "I knew what my parents were going to say before they said it because my parents' marriage had been really bad and I knew the big threat was they were going to get separated or divorced. I always knew it was there. I just burst out crying but the first thing I thought about, which I still feel terrible about, is that my dad would be moving out. I thought, 'Well, at least now I won't have to set the table for four people.' Then I felt all alone. It was almost the end of the world which sounds very melodramatic but I felt everything was falling apart."

The majority of people I spoke with said that even though they had known for a long time that something was amiss with their parents' marriage it was a terrible shock when they were actually confronted with the separation. As Annette describes her experience she was quite able to comprehend the information. She had been expecting this but it was still a shock when her dad finally told her: "I was really upset. They used to fight a lot and my mom would go off in the car for a couple of hours. I was always afraid she would never come back but she always did. I took it pretty well because I knew they weren't getting along at all. I thought it would be better for both of them and for us kids. We had been through a lot of hard times because we had to watch how they fought and didn't get along at all. At first, I was really upset about it because it just sort of shocked me, but then I was okay. It took me a while but I grew out of my days of being upset."

It seems that this initial shock wears off rapidly. Margaret had known for several years that one day her parents might separate. She had even prepared herself for the event. But still she was shocked and not prepared to handle the details of the actual moment: "I was 16 years old. I had a friend go through it. I always felt, 'Oh, wow! She must be going through really hard stuff.' I couldn't believe how she came through it really easily. So I thought to myself, 'Oh, wow! I know my parents are splitting up — something's really going on and I don't know what I'm going to do.' I talked to my friend a lot. Then suddenly it happened. I think I was so shocked when it did happen that I was brain-washed. My mother told me absolutely everything that was going on, and as far as I'm concerned, nobody should know. The relationship with my father was just terrific from 8-16. My mother ruined that. She said, 'You know your father isn't all what you think he is.' She started telling me what he was doing. I just didn't know what to do. All I could do was just sit there and listen to her and believe her. What else could I do? I was just so shocked at the things that you hear about somebody who you really, really loved that much. All of a sudden he wasn't that perfect. It just sort of happened overnight. My mother was very upset and very unstable. She was telling me everything and expecting me to deal with it. I turned around to my father and he didn't know how to respond. He beat me up a couple of times and I tried to ask him his side of the story. He sort of turned me off. Then the next day he got real mad and he started throwing things around and stuff. The next thing I knew he was being kicked out. He made phone calls saying my grandparents didn't want me to live there. They wouldn't want me to go and visit them ever. I didn't know where I was at.

He said my grandparents didn't ever want me to be there again and that they never wanted to see me again, because I believed what my mother said. I practically went nuts. I just couldn't believe it because my grandparents have always been so good to us kids, all three of us."

The confusion which Margaret describes so well may not be such a bad thing, especially if feeling apart and out of it protects you from becoming too involved. Margaret's mother seemed to want her to take sides, but being somewhat detached allowed her to approach her father. Unfortunately, he was unable to respond initially because he saw Margaret as being aligned with her mother. Feeling like a detached observer, or experiencing a sense of "this can't really be happening to me", can sometimes help a person get through the initial shock and pain. Although the shock wears off, the feeling of being apart or detached may last for up to a year. The adolescents in the group who were able to separate themselves from the situation seemed to be able to understand what was happening better. They were able to see clearly each parent's difficulties and each parent's point of view.

It may be hard to remain an impartial observer when you are just as affected by the family upheaval as your parents are. Your parents may appear confused and upset, and you will want to comfort them. Some people found themselves sitting up until two or three in the morning trying to help their mother or father sort things out. Looking back on it they agreed it might have been better to get one of their parent's friends, a close relative or a trained counsellor to talk with that parent. Margaret's advice now is, "Don't listen. Say, 'I don't want to hear any more.' It's intriguing and interesting that your mom tells you everything and trusts you, but forget it 'cause when it comes to your dad you're out in the cold. I'm angry at my mother for doing that. It makes me mad." How unfortunate that Margaret's mother tried to get Margaret to take sides. This not only pushed Margaret away from her father but also turned her anger towards her mother.

A very similar situation happened with John and his father: "My parents told us on my sister's birthday. It was pretty evil of them to do that. It was there. I just didn't see it. Like, my mother the summer before had a nervous breakdown that lasted a few months. I didn't know how to explain what was going on. I went on a trip with my dad out West. It was a bad mistake 'cause he kept telling me how evil my mother was. When I came back I wanted to stay with him. It was kind of foolish. It was a stupid thing to do. After the trip I kind of hated my mother and when I realized what he was doing I hated my father."

The initial reactions of Margaret, John and Barbara may not be at all familiar to you. While they do represent a fairly typical kind of reaction, what you experience may seem completely different. You may find some similarities, but, of course, each person's experience is uniquely their own. Two people, of all those I talked with, said that the actual fact of the separation came as a surprise as well as a shock. They had no premonition that this was going to happen. Dawn says, "After my mother told us that they were splitting up we didn't really know what it meant. Like, we thought they'll get back together pretty soon. We'd see our dad again and he'll live with us again. But after a while we realized it was for good, and that we were going to have to live with that and there wasn't anything us kids could do about it."

It is not uncommon for younger children to wish

that their parents would get together again. Some feel that if their parents stop loving each other they will stop loving their children too. Sometimes they even try to arrange meetings between their parents. So we can understand how Dawn, who had just turned 11, found it difficult to accept her parents' separation. Harold, however, seems to have been caught completely off guard: "I came home from school and my mother wasn't there. My mother had moved about two miles away. I had no premonition about anything that was going to happen like this but it did and after about six months she came back to the house. My father was upset. They used to get up in the morning and argue over the stupidest things. When I tried to talk it out with my father he said, 'I can't live in the basement for the rest of my life,' which is quite understandable. He moved out with his mother, my grandmother. After about four months my sister was quite a problem to my mother and finally she just told her to get out, so my sister left and moved in with my father and grandmother. Things were getting along okay, I guess. There weren't any hassles or anything. My mother got fed up and asked me to leave. She didn't ask me. She didn't even tell me. She went to the basement and grabbed a suitcase and came up the stairs and threw it at me, knocked the breakfast table right over — the food and dishes and everything — all over the place. So I ended up moving in with my father and my sister and my grandmother. It was like a dream world. I didn't believe it."

After the shock, some people experienced a sense of relief. For some the relief came right away; for others, after a day or two. For Michael, the separation meant an end to the terrible fights, sometimes physical, between his parents: "I was at summer camp and when

I got back my mother had moved with my two sisters to a new apartment. There was no, like, real violence at home but there was constant arguing. I can remember it was kind of building up over the years. I was kind of young but I knew something was inevitably happening and that there was a possibility of divorce. We left and it was much happier. There was less tension, less pressure. It would get ugly before when my parents tried to influence us against the other parent. I loved both my parents although I suppose I was closer to my mother. I guess we would feel protective of my mother during heated arguments and the times when they got kind of physical and he would be stronger so my mother would be overpowered and hurt. I was just more relieved to be away from the tension.''

Those people who told me that the reason for the separation was an alcohol problem for one of their parents often experienced a great deal of relief. Ted explains how difficult things were for his family prior to the separation: "I was not really involved. I knew it was going to happen sooner or later. It grew and grew and grew. My father is an alcoholic and I thought I'd lose my father. It really never bothered me — just the fighting and being up all night because of my dad's problem. But I found it very hard when I first saw my father leave. But I had accepted his alcoholism. I knew it would happen because my older brothers would throw him out or call the police night after night, five or six days a week for years. Separation was good more or less. It was more or less of a relief.''

But family life does not have to be so obviously upsetting in order for someone to feel relieved. Jill recalls: "When I was 14 my father left for another woman — typical reason! It was a relief more than anything. It had always been tense. Always screaming and yelling. I love them both very much but when it was all three of us together — I'm an only child — it was tense. Now that he's gone the house is very relaxed. They'd been on a vacation together to Spain. When they came back my mother sat me down and told me he was leaving. I felt relief and nothing more. I was glad I didn't feel bad about being glad: I felt great about being glad. It didn't bother me at all. It made me treat him a little differently at first because he had hurt my mother."

Following the initial shock and relief of tension many people in the group felt sad as they realized the loss of one parent to the family. Some people said it was almost as if the parent who left had died except that the pain and hurt of loss came back every time they visited that parent. A lot of things changed for Sally because her father stayed on in the family home while she moved out with her mother: "We moved out, my mother, my brother and I. At first it was strange not having my father around. My mother was quite upset. For about six months I continued to want to go and be with my father."

Gordon's parents never actually sat down and explained they were separating, so he did not experience shock but gradually came to feel intensely the loss of his mother. "We sort of thought she wasn't really leaving, she was going away on a kind of trip. Eventually it began to sink in. You don't realize that anyone is going away forever even though that may be the case. There was something missing. The presence of someone that you need isn't there."

These three feelings of shock, relief and loss, in this order, seem to be a fairly common occurrence. An exception to this was the experience of Jerry, who felt embarrassed when he thought of having to tell people that his parents were separating: "It was a sudden type of thing and my parents came to myself and my brother and they just told us right out that they were getting divorced. I sort of felt this was going to happen even though there was no talk of it. I could see the way the marriage was going that something had to change and I figured divorce would be the thing. My father had thrown out my oldest brother, my mother's favorite, while she was on vacation in England. When she got back she was very upset. He took it very badly that she wanted a divorce. For some reason it didn't bother me at the time. Then there was this awful scene at my grandparents' with my parents each wanting us to go with the other one. I had to make a choice and that was hard. It's kind of hard to remember what actually happened. I was feeling pretty bad. I didn't know what I was going to do. I figured I had to go to school and tell my friends — I felt kind of an embarrassment at having to tell people." After he told one close friend, Jerry found it easier to tell his other friends as well.

Bob explains how he went from being embarrassed to being quite proud of having gone through his parents' separation and of being able to cope with it maturely. "My parents started off being quite religious. They had quite an ideal marriage. Everyone thought so. I did too. But after my father's father died it affected him. He realized what a miserable life his father had. I guess it kind of scared him, but he started to change his lifestyle. He broke away from the church. He started taking art classes in sculpture and things like that. He got to be good friends with this teacher. In the fall my parents would occasionally raise their voices, which was quite uncommon. Well, Christmas Eve we didn't go to church, which is unusual, and I cried. I was at a stage when I didn't cry very much and for some reason on Christmas Eve I cried and I couldn't figure out why I was so sad. But I think I could sense my parents trying to hold something together that just wasn't going to go. During the spring there were about a dozen outbursts between my parents. My mom would end up crying and none of us knew why. I remember how stunned I was when my mom told me that she and my father were going to a marriage counsellor. My dad left in June at the end of the school year. One afternoon in late May, the whole family got together and sat in the living-room and they told us about the possible separation in June. It was no news to me. My dad started crying and my mother was feeling quite self-righteous. So that's when I felt sorry for my father. I remember in June when my parents were separated I was embarrassed. I didn't want my close friends to know. Now it's funny 'cause I'm proud that my parents are divorced. I don't know why — I feel you get a sort of strength from the whole thing. The initial shock took place in June and took almost a month to die down just to the beginning of July. I got a job that year and I stayed away from home. I was washing pots in a kitchen at a summer camp and I think it was good. It made the separation take a back seat because it was the worst job I have ever had in my life."

I think that Bob did a very sensible thing in taking that summer job. He was able to get away from all the tension at home long enough for the initial shock to die down, and the hard physical labor allowed him to work out some of his own personal frustration and tension. Likewise, other people in the group said that strenuous physical activity, whether a job or a sport like skiing or hockey, really helped during those first few weeks. It seems that this kind of mental and emotional stress can be worked out to some extent physically. The obvious advantage of a sport or job is that it usually has to be carried out away from home. You may feel you don't want to leave your mother or father alone when they are obviously suffering as much as you. But you may find that you are more able to help your parents when you've put a little temporary distance between yourself and all the turmoil at home.

The exhausting and exhilarating sport of cross-country running prevented Barry from getting locked into the anger and resentment that he felt building up in himself: "My parents are separated. About five years ago my father found a girlfriend. He was about 50 and he kept it a secret. Nobody knew and we seemed to be the happiest family on the street. I never expected anything like that of my father. Then one year when we were on vacation we stopped by a store and my father bought an incredibly beautiful dress for his secretary because she was — some excuse. My mother started to become suspicious. She pried it out of him. Everybody in the family knew for about a week except me. I knew something was wrong because everyone was upset and everybody was frightened, but I didn't know what was wrong. A week later they told me — I didn't feel too surprised. I guess I was shocked and frightened. It took maybe a week for it to settle in. After that I had very destructive feelings. I wanted to hurt somebody. I wanted to hurt somebody and I guess I had to get out my aggressions by physical labor. I joined cross-country running and just ran my guts out."

Marion explains how important it was for her to separate herself from her parents' concerns even before the separation. In doing so she found herself taking a more responsible place in the family. Her job, as she saw it, was to continue supporting her mother and her older sister but to keep herself emotionally separate from the problem between her parents. Despite this attitude, Marion still felt shocked when her parents finally decided to separate: "I'm 18 years old. When I was about 13 or 14 my parents were going through the usual type of marital problems of fighting and just arguments almost every day after work, or something. My mother wasn't working. She would always try to do her best around the house and everything but my father was never satisfied. He would say that this wasn't clean or she was being lazy. My mother got very upset, naturally. She mentioned to my dad that she would like a divorce and my dad begged her to stay and convinced her. It was a little subdued for a while, then reached a peak. Then my parents didn't fight anymore and everything seemed to be going well. My case is different from all the others, I think, because my sister had a severe mental illness for about 4-5 years. It started when I was 14. There are a few theories that it started as the result of my parents. Anyway, it caused a lot of tension in the house. My dad was under a lot of tension. He had these ideals for his daughters to reach. My sister had an accident also, so she was destroying all his ideals for what a young woman should be. My mother got really upset so I ended up being the pillar of strength. I took pride in this. I didn't let it affect me. I tried to separate myself from the problem and for a long time I did and I got along quite well. My sister went off to university and the tensions eased. But one weekend there seemed to be something strange going on in the house and I felt it. I sensed something in the air. They didn't seem on the surface upset but they wouldn't talk to me. I didn't really want to know — I think it was subconscious fear. After I came back they sat me down, which was very rare for my parents 'cause my father never really made a point of talking to me. I guessed then but I stayed quiet, and they told me they were going to get a separation. I didn't really react that strongly. But I didn't know why, so I assumed that one of them had an affair. So I asked my father and he told me he did and I was shocked."

Keeping out of your parents' problems is not without dangers: when a person begins to withdraw from one situation, it can sometimes lead to withdrawal from others. Jim saw this happen with his brother: "I'm glad they got divorced because now I'm more independent. I don't know why they really got divorced but I was a bit upset at first. We moved for three months to my aunt and uncle's and then into a condominium. But my older brother — he's second oldest — he took it kind of bad. He had a lot of friends but when we moved he became a sort of recluse. Only thing is, when my parents got divorced, back then, no one got divorced. It's common now. It was hard to believe." It seems that Jim's brother kept his distance from his parents' concerns but, because of embarrassment, was unable to share his own troubles with his friends. In this instance, it might have helped him if he had gotten into a new outside activity. One warning sign you might look for, indicating that you are becoming too withdrawn, is if you spend a lot of time alone listening to music or watching television, especially if you have not been in the habit of doing so previously.

What happens if you are unable to keep yourself apart from the concerns of your parents? Some people found that a great deal of anger built up inside them, and if they had no outlet for this anger it turned into bitterness and resentment toward one or both parents. For Elizabeth, this was like a battle going on inside her over her loyalty to her mother or to her father. "I've never known, to this day, why they separated. I had heard my mother and father fighting in the next room for I had a bedroom beside them. I came home one day and found a 'For Sale' sign in front of my house. I was walking home with a friend and she says 'I never knew you were selling your house.' I went into my mother and said 'Hey, what's the 'For Sale' sign for?' She says, 'Well, we're moving.' She never gave me a reason or why. When all the furniture was out of the house and everything was cleared out except for the rugs, my father and mother sat down and my mother explained that they could not get along with each other. My sister was only seven years old so it was up to me to keep on the tough side. It's just the initial shock. I was aware something was happening. I was very angry inside and I took my anger out on my little sister and if I look back I wish I never did that. I ran away from home five or six times. I'd always come back. It was very silly. I never got far. I took sides: I'd say, 'Well, my father's at fault for this and my mother's at fault for that.' I really shouldn't have. At first, I was a brat and a bully. I was not loving. I never knew what it was going to be like. I had no understanding.''

Sometimes, in their own anger and hurt, parents behave rather badly in these first few very difficult weeks. One parent who feels hurt may try to strike back at the other parent. It may, at times, seem very childish and immature, as if the parent is saying, "You hurt me, so I'm going to hurt you back." In this kind of situation it may be very difficult indeed to retain a somewhat distant perspective. Laurie found her own shock turned rapidly into bitterness and anger at what she saw as unfair and hurtful behavior on the part of her father. "At the beginning it was shock. The first time I had any thoughts was in my last year of public school. Now I wish it had happened then instead of waiting. Our family relationship slowly deteriorated. I think my parents' biggest problems were not being able to sit down and talk with each other. It's pretty rough growing up in your adolescent years and listening to your parents talking about how they wished they'd never got married and how they always wished they never had you kids. There's four children in my family. I'm the only girl and I've got two older brothers and one younger. I really believe it hit me the hardest. My father started taking off on us all the time. He was out to all hours and we really didn't know what was going on. We could never sleep at night because of my parents' constant bickering. That's all you could hear. Finally, my eldest brother figured it out: he told my mother. We kids had seen him going to Mary's apartment quite a number of times. I can't remember the exact situation of how my father left. He up and left one day. My mother was really afraid to do anything. My father came back two days in a row and cleared the house out. He left my mother with a bed for herself and her clothes. He took the color T.V. He took all the living-room furniture except the piano which was a gift to my mother from her mother. Things were pretty bad for us. The shock began to turn to bitterness towards my father.''

Although many of the people in the group spoke of an intense anger, often at the way one parent was behaving, this anger did not usually come so soon after the parents' separation. Anger and how adolescents in the group dealt with their angry feelings is described in the next chapter. But to summarize how the adolescents I talked with reacted, at first, to their parents' separation, they were shocked — but somehow not surprised. Many were also relieved that some action was finally being taken to stop the ever-present family feud and tension, some people were embarrassed, while others developed conflicting loyalties. After one parent leaves most people begin to feel not only the loss of this parent but the loss of family togetherness and wholeness.

ADVICE ON INITIAL REACTIONS:

For adolescents
1 Shock is normal.
2 You don't have to tell everyone, but do tell someone — anyone you trust — about it. Talking out loud helps to make things more real, less confusing.
3 Get into an activity: participate in a sport, join a group or take on a new job.
4 Support your parents by helping around the house, not by talking for hours about the details.

For parents
1 Tell your children together, if possible — no lurid details, please.
2 Allow your adolescent some distance, but be available to respond to his or her need for affection.
3 Insist that normal household tasks and routines carry on.
4 Don't allow skipping off school or extra-curricular activities because your child says he or she is too upset to go.

3
There are No Sides in a Divorce.

"The best thing to do is accept it. The odds are they are never going to get back together." All but one of the people in the group had completely accepted the fact within two weeks to a month after their parents' separation. But accepting the fact doesn't necessarily mean that everything is suddenly fine again. Some of the most painful feelings occur after the shock has worn off and the permanence of the loss of the family as it was sinks in. How does one cope with accepting that a separation is permanent? "Our family had to adjust at first when he finally left," says Ted. "But now I think we've gotten through that stage, and we're all used to it. I'm more or less trying to help other teenagers now. I've talked to lots of people where their fathers just start to drink a little too much but it's starting to grow. I talk about my experience and that seems to help. It's hard for a teenager to accept some things, especially if their father's an alcoholic. It bothers me sometimes that I had no one to talk to. This is my one regret."

Some people noted real changes for the better after

the separation and so had less difficulty accepting it as permanent. Abby and Jill found that their fathers seemed happier. It seemed easier to communicate with them afterwards, but Abby experienced some awkward moments at first: "I was glad after they separated because of the fights but I felt guilty about not visiting and scared of visiting my dad. But he's really changed. He wants to be with us and became like a real father. Now they're totally separate people." Jill says: "So now I live with my mother and see my father every couple of weeks. He is living with another woman who has a little girl. We get along just beautifully. When I'm over there it's really happy and there's no tension at all. Everything is so much better. The hardest part is when I'm with my mom and she starts talking about things that my dad has done or what she thinks about him and I don't know quite what to do. I refuse to take sides but I also like to support the other person while they're cutting them down. But sometimes I feel like saying things like 'You're wrong, my dad's gotten much nicer. He's really a great guy.' But I don't. I think her feelings about him are her problem. There's nothing I can do to change that. She's a grown woman. When I was 13 I seriously considered leaving home at 16. But now I'm 16 and I'm looking forward to spending the next six or seven years with her as I go through university. I've just been brought so much closer to the two of them because of their separation than I could have hoped for."

Of course, not everyone finds the adjustment easy. I mentioned earlier that sometimes the first feelings of shock and relief often turn into anger. And whether they're angry at the situation, their parents or society for legal and court difficulties, the anger people feel is, at times, intense. When you are feeling angry and helpless, the easiest and quickest way to get rid of some of the anger is to dump it on someone close to you, like a parent. This leads to choosing sides and usually to putting all the blame on one parent, often the parent who is not living with you. This anger, which starts as a flame of resentment, can grow into a blaze of rage if fueled by conversations with one parent and exclusion of the other parent. Laurie took sides against her father: "I became bitter towards my father during the whole thing. I wanted it all in the past. I was glad and relieved when they had their legal divorce. I was also mad at what my mom got stuck with — no money and everything. Overall, it was mostly bitterness and hate. I felt through the whole thing pity for my mother. Now after it, I think it was the best thing that ever happened, not staying together, and overall it was the best thing for all of us."

Sally's bitterness to her father grew over time and seems to be correlated with a gradual shifting of loyalty to her mother: "We'd visit my father and come home talking about everything that he'd given us and that mother hadn't given us — sort of saying she wasn't being a good mother. For about six months we told Mother constantly that we wanted to go to live with my father. She kept telling us he was lying to us. Now that he's moved in with his girlfriend he's stopped being so nice to us. He won't put any effort towards us. He won't pick us up at our house. We have to meet him far away. He didn't pick up any of the negative feelings or anything that went wrong was someone else's fault. We were all stupid and dumb and he was perfect. I was confused — I didn't know if I had a father or not. Gradually I saw my father less and less, finally just for celebrations. I was beginning to realize my father's attitude. I got angry. So a positive came out of the whole ordeal. I learned how to stand up for myself. My dad still throws negative shots at us but we can handle them. We are living in a new house and are quite happy." I think that Sally shows maturity in continuing to keep contact with her father even if it is less frequent than before. She is able to see his faults and weaknesses and not totally reject him because of them. It is a normal part of adolescent growth to come to gradually recognize that your parents aren't "perfect". Your parents, like everyone else in this world, have weaknesses. Sometimes, when parents separate, this recognition of parents as real people comes suddenly and is not part of a gradual learning. That can be hard to deal with. You may find yourself resisting this change, wanting to go back to an earlier, happier time. You may find yourself rejecting one parent totally, wanting to have nothing to do with him or her.

Even if you struggle to remain objective and see your parents for what they are — hurt, confused and, at times, guilty individuals — you can sometimes get "sucked in" by the continuing battle. Bob found that his mother was not seeing him clearly but that he represented his father in the house: "I've never harbored any malice toward my father or my mother, for that matter. During the divorce, my mother was sort of a victim and she was sort of self-righteous. Ever since she sort of magnified her feelings. She enjoys getting sympathy which I don't think is necessary. I went away to camp, at first, and by the time I got back all the pain had sort of drained away. But I got into some vicious arguments with my mother by defending my father. I'm a lot like him and I sort of represented him in the house. So she would kind of take her anger out on me. There was side-taking with my sister and brother too. When there's an argument I can run rings around her logically. In the end she gets irrational. In the last two years I haven't missed my dad so much. But I miss talking with him in an adult fashion. This separation, strange as it sounds, has definitely strengthened both my relationship to my mother and my father. I started feeling strong, like I'd won a battle. I feel like it's a status symbol."

Bob's mother is not the only parent who acted like this. I think that this is one of the saddest things that can happen in a separation: in two out of five cases in the group, one or both parents were locked in a bitter struggle. The adolescents in these families felt very angry at their parents for trying to get them to take sides. Often, as with Bob's mother, the anger backfires on the parent who is most bitter or who makes the most snide remarks. Margaret suggests you can help a parent who is caught up in this way by ignoring the comments: "Don't listen. Say, 'I don't want to hear any more.' It's intriguing and interesting that Mom tells you everything and trusts you but forget it 'cause when it comes to Dad you're out in the cold. Don't listen. I'm angry at my mom for doing that. It makes me mad." John describes how an angry, resentful parent who really wants to be reassured and cared for can end up with less affection: "It's a big mistake, especially like right after your parents split up to lose contact with one of them right away. Because even without knowing it the other parent, through their own hate, turns you away. I was confused and under the influence of my father. I started to say things about my mother which were unfair. I can see that now. Now I'm angry at my father. He won't admit he has a problem. When I realized what my father was doing I got really down on life. I hated school and I was thinking of suicide. My mother tries to be objective but she can't. I was also going to school and doing a lot of standard things and I was enjoying myself. It has worked out better. Things were tense before they split up. So like, in a way, I'm glad they split up. I think there was a lot of sick things going on there." John got caught up in taking sides but the tragedy is that he felt guilty, responsible and depressed when he realized what had happened to him. Sometimes, I think parents who let this happen to themselves and their children are not really aware of the consequences. John advises that if you find yourself in circumstances like his, "Talk to someone totally impartial. Don't take sides. One goes to one side and jumps across to the other as soon as they do something wrong." Annette recalls how she was able to avoid taking sides: "My father's adultery hurt me. But I feel if I acted upset or rude to my mother or father it wouldn't be doing any good because it's not going to change their minds. It would make them feel like they were ruining my life so I just went along with it. Moving away was hard. When I saw other people going through divorce I was glad we still see our father. He hurt me once when he put Mom down. I got really scared of him. He's got a really bad temper. I don't really mind now because I see that my mom's happier and Dad's happier."

Another tragic situation that can occur when parents try to get you to take sides is that you may find yourself avoiding the parent you visit so you won't have to listen to him or her putting your other parent down. Michael would have liked to have much more contact with his father: "Soon after they separated I began visiting my father. There was tension there and I was getting caught in the middle. They'd both ask questions about the other one. They'd make little snide remarks about each other. I remember being hurt at times, like my *bar mitzvah*. It was quiet and there were no hassles so I left it alone. It was hard to forget the past impressions of my parents' fighting. Even if I didn't have all that much in common with my father I still would like to have had him when I was younger but now that I'm older I guess because I got along without him I feel maybe a slight resentment because I couldn't have him when I needed him. I guess now I know that you should visit your other parent regardless of what the parent you're living with says. Because eventually that parent will understand that a kid needs to see the other parent. The kid shouldn't be punished for the divorce."

Marion also thinks it helps to "separate yourself. It seems wrong to say this but you have to because it can tear you apart. Try to be an objective helper." Elizabeth adds: "Have lots of understanding and love for both parents. If you can't see your father at least try and retain a parental relationship. Don't pick sides. There are no sides in a divorce."

One in five people felt no particular anger. One of these was Karen, whose parents decided that each would retain parental responsibility by agreeing to joint custody. Although her parents argue at times over the financial arrangements, "I feel pretty lucky because most other people I know, they just live with one of their parents and their other parent lives far away but since my parents live two blocks away it's almost like without a separation. I don't really like it that they're living different ways but still they're happier and it's easier now. I'm used to being brought up both ways."

So even this "ideal" arrangement has its problems and requires adjustments. Financial arrangements and the reduced amount of money available after the separation can, indeed, spark angry feelings. Marion tries hard not to be influenced by what seems to be a miserly attitude on her father's part: "My father moved out and in with his girlfriend. I felt really sorry for my mother because she had the humiliation all those years and just when she thought things were getting better and just when things did start straightening out in the family then she got this blow in the face. Everything was going so well financially. Now it's changed around. It's really hard not to think that you're getting ripped off. He's always saying how poor he is. But he's rich and my mother has to work so hard. My mother never complains, but it's hard not to get really resentful. I think you benefit in a lot of ways, having to face fears of being alone and because of this experience, my mother and I feel that we are doing the right thing and from that we get a sense of satisfaction. Sometimes you get to the stage where you're looking for pity. It's just an excuse for acting in strange ways. So you can get sympathy. I really had to watch out for that. That was only a stage though. My sister's reaction was very different from mine. I've accepted it. It was almost an adventure. I think it's the best thing for my mother."

Even if your parents don't force you to take sides, you may find yourself feeling resentful towards one parent. Jerry has managed to work out some of this resentment. He is fortunate that his mother and father understand and want him to see both of them: "At first my father was working and it was strange to come home from school and nobody would be there. Waking in the morning and your mother not there is hard. I kind of got to blaming my mother for all the extra work we had to do, cleaning and washing. I still feel a resentment towards her even though I speak to her now. I feel you can't hate a person all your life. You have to see their side of the story too. My mother thought, at one point, my father was brainwashing me in not wanting to come and see her. She was wrong. He was pushing us to go and see her — he thought I shouldn't act that way toward her. Finally she stopped fighting. If I don't want to call her I don't have to. Well, that's exactly what I wanted and now I call her up and I speak to her when I want to. I get along good with her. I found out that if I wanted to abuse my privileges I could, but I'd be only hurting myself. I'm glad I stuck by my father. I don't think he would have made it without my brother and I. I think a child has to do that." Jim, who also lives with his father, had to make a lot of adjustments, including moving to a new neighborhood and dealing with his mother's remarriage. He seems to feel that in the end his parents did the right thing. "We moved and I started meeting lots of different people. There were a lot of people whose parents were divorced and separated and the kids were all completely different from kids that come from normal families. We'd talk about how dumb to what's going on around them kids with two parents are. My mom was happier. By the next year she was completely changed. It was like she discovered herself. I'd go visit her and we could talk and she'd take me all kinds of places that kids my own age never go. When you need a friend, she's a friend too. After two years I had adjusted completely. I'd see my mom on weekends and be with my own family, my brother and my dad. My mom got married again and doesn't have as much time. That affected me. My school work really fell off. I became too independent too fast. I was spending too much time with girls. My brother started getting into crime. I think it was just the friends he hung around with. I'm the only guy in the family who hasn't been into crime. I guess I learned from my brother's mistakes. I love both my parents deeply but it's to my benefit that they got divorced. I've got a mother, I've got a father, but they just don't live together. I'm the same person I was years ago except that I don't live with both my parents — but maybe I'm more independent."

Jim mentions that his brother was getting into crime. This can happen if a person becomes very angry: he begins to take his anger out on society, not just on his immediate family. Barry thinks that when you become angry you "look for a release, some way of expressing yourself." This is what happened to Joel. Fortunately, he found out what was happening before any permanent damage was done: "My sister was angry at my dad. One day we had a fight and I said I couldn't really condemn him since he'd never done anything to hurt anybody personally. My sister told me my father had wanted me aborted before I was born. This disturbed me. I felt I wasn't wanted and I felt generally funny. I wasn't able to relate to the other kids anymore. I couldn't really make them understand what was happening to me. After a while though, things with my father began to look up. I felt a lot better and I began to doubt what my mother told me about my father. I began to notice a strong desire to live with my father. Then in the middle of the night I got a friend of mine and I snuck my mother's car keys and we went joy-riding. We were pulled over by a policeman. My mother talked to them and they didn't press charges. If I did it again I'd stay out of the situation. My big mistake was getting involved." Joel's anger seemed to really start when he began to feel that no one cared, that he was an unwanted child — a burden.

Gordon didn't experience as much anger as Joel, but he felt very rejected when his mother moved out

West. He seems to have withdrawn into himself for a time and was quite depressed: "We began to get used to the situation of living without my mother. My father looked after us as well as he could. He cooked the meals, he took care of us. I'm not complaining, but there's always something missing. In the early stages I wrote to my mother, but gradually the ties were broken — I suppose you can't hang on to parents forever. But I feel I was rejected by my mother and father. They never seem close to me and that makes it hard for me to open up to people. You know, it's a learning experience. I felt isolated and less loved but also learned a great deal from it."

Depression and loneliness can be hard to deal with. Elizabeth found an alternative solution to withdrawing to help with her loneliness: "Later it became a financial battle between my father and mother. I and my sister stayed with my mother and the boys with my father. Usually, until you're 16, the courts put you with your mother. I had regular visits with my father. But then things became a big hassle. As the eldest daughter I was getting pushed around. I would be expected to do things. I was protecting my sister. No one was in the wrong, no one in the right to me. It may sound funny right now but I felt like a ping pong ball. I was tossed from my mother to my father from weekends to week-days and it began to bug me. I got to the point where I'd bottle all my problems up inside me and then I would just hit the roof at anyone who passed my path. I took off my door handle from the outside so my mother and sister couldn't get at me. My mother would bang on the door and I would turn the music on the radio up. I used to have physical fights with my mother — that was wrong. I used to throw furniture around the house and I used to be really annoying to my mother. My mother didn't know what to do with me. I just felt alone. I felt I didn't have a father or a mother — I only had them as a name. I think they should have shown more love and affection toward us — my sister and I. I started doing things, anything to keep me busy: art and crafts, dancing, guitar lessons and junior modelling. I've become a more outgoing person. I've also learned how to have fun without spending a lot of money. I've begun to appreciate that there are a lot of people out there more unfortunate than I am. I think I'm a better person for this experience."

Barry found, as Elizabeth did, that getting the anger out through physical activity prevented his becoming more bitter and resentful: "I began to worry about my father. He's had yet another girlfriend and is screwing around even more. I don't know. But the thing that cured me was physical labor. I guess you have to survive. Talking to my sisters really helped. Our family really began to work together and share things. I still have some anger at my father for not getting the proper divorce and pretending to be married to his girlfriend — I mean, it's just the lying. I'd rather see them married and my mother getting the proper alimony. It's a lack of responsibility and it's given me a lack of respect for my father. I admire my mother and what she's done."

Barry found talking to his sisters helped him deal with his anger. Annette also feels that talking about your anger and depression can help dispel these feelings: "Talk to your best friend. Talk to someone. Don't worry. There's not much you can do. Your depression only makes your parents feel worse and they feel bad enough as it is."

Jeff lost not only his father but his brother and sister when he decided to move to another city with his mother. This loss was made even more painful and lonely because his mother was often absent for business reasons. Jeff had to adjust to the change from a family of five to being on his own much of the time. He keeps thinking over the difficulties at the time his parents separated: "Personally, I don't have any hard feelings to my mother or my father. The worst part was trying to decide who to live with. I came with my mother and I miss my brother and sister. My mother goes away often and I sit down alone to dinner or watch T.V. and I'm lonely. The worst time was when my father broke into my mother's house. You see, he never really accepted the fact. But they fight and it's just like a spider's web. You get caught in the middle. With my parents it's still going on. It would be a real load off everybody's mind if they finally just said, 'Goodbye'. One day my father was taking nerve pills. He doesn't drink but he was upset and a friend gave him a drink. The drugs got mixed up: he was too high. He came home and sat downstairs crying. My brother, sister and I were all in bed. It's really a difficult thing to see, your father crying. He was just sitting there with his hands between his knees weeping like a baby. I was scared to come down but I did and tried to comfort him. But he had thoughts of grabbing a gun and going to shoot my mother. He drove over to my mother's house — she wouldn't let him in so he broke a window. I think he must have hit her. She was just in a frenzy and I'm not too sure but I think she had a male guest. My father took the truck and started playing bumper cars with this guy's car. But the police came and took him away to jail for the night. It looked very bad for both their careers. My mother got a peace bond and my father couldn't come near her. My mother came and got us and took us to her friend's place and we were hiding out. I was really pissed off. I didn't know where I was at. But eventually we got back with my dad. I talked to friends. It was hard, though, having to make big decisions at a young age. It's still hard on Christmas trying to be with both of them. But they're getting used to it. Once you get by the first part, anything seems easy. You know it will never get back to normal but things become quiet. You have to learn to live with it as best you can."

Joel feels that a pet can help to lift the spirits of a person who's feeling very alone: "A cat or a dog is a kind of therapy. Because you have this animal and it's like a child of your own. You can bring this animal up yourself to behave in a way you want it to behave. This is what I did with my cat." What I think Joel means about making an animal "behave in a way you want it to behave" is that helping an animal learn to control its behavior can help you gain a sense of competence and control over the confusion that surrounds a divorce.

As I have said before, everyone's own experience differs slightly from others', but generally the adolescents in the group went through feeling stages of shock, relief, sense of loss, acceptance, anger, loneliness and depression, and final adjustment. Barbara describes these later stages very well: "My mind got really messed up. Being a teenager, you're going through a lot of other problems like meeting new friends at different schools. At home there were fights. I'd want to turn around and run to Daddy — but Daddy doesn't live here anymore. I did that a couple of times when things got really bad, I ran to Dad, but always came back to Mom because I lived with Mom sort of thing. I started getting the feeling of people hating me. I was really angry at being different. At that time you never heard about separation or divorce like you do now — I wanted it under the rug. I got angry at Mom for asking me questions about Dad when she didn't want Dad to know about her: it wasn't fair. I felt Dad was being cheated. The bond between my mom and I practically evaporated and I was really angry, especially because my mom was having an affair. I was really confused. Here I **was**, loving one parent and hating the other and yet that parent was really the one who was best for me. I finally realized that Mom can't love Dad and that there's bound to be a few problems in any teenager's life. My parents' divorce was really best all the way round."

I asked some people, what they would say to someone who was going through these feelings of anger, depression and loneliness. Jerry said: "I'd probably tell him not to worry about it. I'd reassure him that in time it will be O.K. Worry about yourself. I worried about my mother and she's fine. Take care of yourself." Laurie responded: "Try and talk things out with people and your parents, try to understand what they've gone through. I thought too much of myself and didn't think too much of how my parents were feeling. I'd try to give both parents a chance. It's pretty hard to stay on both parents' side."

Jerry and Laurie seem to be contradicting each other. Actually, I think they are both right by suggesting that over-involvement with one's parents can be just as troublesome as not caring and only worrying about yourself. It seems that one must strive to keep a balance between these two positions. As Abby says, "Try to stay mutual between them, and try to keep your own identity for what you feel, instead of feeling badly for other people all the time, trying to do what you think they want. Stay neutral and give support to both parents. Assume more responsibilities than you had before. It really helped me. Talk to someone outside if your mom says bad things about your dad and vice versa. Don't be too hard on your parents or yourself. Don't be so sensitive — you'll get hurt. But don't wall yourself off either." You may be feeling, after reading this advice, that it sounds too difficult and too complicated to be believed. Take courage: most people come through these various feeling stages pretty well and some people, like Margaret, feel they're better people for having done so: "I've pulled myself through and I've become a stronger person."

ADVICE ABOUT LATER FEELINGS:

For adolescents
1 Feeling angry or sad is not unusual.
2 Try not to take your anger out on those around you. Get it out in physical activity. Take on more responsibilities.
3 If you are getting into trouble at school or outside the home you may need more help with your anger than you're getting. Ask to talk to someone outside the family.
4 Try to ignore parents' remarks about each other.

For parents
1 The anger that you express may end up back on your doorstep.
2 Help your teenager to express anger verbally.
3 Your adolescents will almost certainly miss your ex-partner: this is no reflection on your ability to care for your children as a single parent. Don't expect too much of yourself all at once.

4
What Really Happened?

You may have asked yourself, "What happened to my parents' marriage? They must have loved each other at one time. What went wrong?" Most adolescents have some idea of what went wrong towards the end. Only one person in the group was not aware of the final reason for his parents' separation. Adultery was the most common reason for separation, followed by constant disagreement and fighting, alcoholism, emotional incompatibility and a change in one parent's personality, in that order. Reasons for divorce changed the order slightly with further deterioration in the parents' relationship after separation being given as the most frequent reason. Also, a wish to remarry was often the impetus to start divorce proceedings; as was a continuing alcoholic problem for one of the parents. These were the causes that the adolescents gave me, not necessarily the official justification which appeared on the divorce papers.

At first, not everyone knew what the real underlying causes were. I think most parents try to protect their children if they feel the truth will be too painful. They may feel that to air their differences or to hurl accusations at one another in front of their children is not going to help anyone. I wondered just how much parents should tell adolescents. Some of the group discussed how much of the truth, as the parents know it, they should share with their teenagers. Sharon says that for her the whole truth is very important: "We're working on communications. I'd be very upset if they hid things from me and I found out something later."

Margaret feels parents could be slightly more judicious in how much they tell: "I don't think you should color the truth nor go right into details. I think you should say as much as you know in terms of the child's future." Jill thinks, "Parents should be responsible for giving both sides. If they were married there must have been some redeeming qualities." I agree, but it may not always be possible for a parent who is hurting to see both sides clearly. You may find yourself with two different impressions of what really caused the separation. If this happens, Annette says, "Kids don't know what to believe. If you're getting double messages, say, 'Tell me the truth or stop lying to everybody.' It's a family thing and everybody has a right to know."

Nancy remembers that she was able to understand the situation long before the separation occurred and she cautions that knowing too many details may be worse than not knowing the truth: "When I was young, before the separation, I had to find it out myself. I figured it out. He was doing something with another lady, I wasn't clear what at the time. My mother hated this lady. She was Dad's secretary. My mom was saying bad things about this lady — I just sort of figured it out. My mom said he was sleeping at the factory, so I just had to figure out why. Later I went with Mother and talked to a counsellor. Mom would say things about him committing adultery and all that. I asked her if she was trying to tell me not to love him, that he was bad. She'd say that she wasn't saying not to love him. I'd say, 'Well, that's how it sounds to me and frankly I don't want to hear it.' "

What if parents continue to resist telling you the truth? I've talked with adolescents outside our group who told me that they pushed for the truth and found out about homosexuality or, in some instances, about sexual perversion on the part of one parent. This kind of information, while not damaging in itself, takes time to get used to, and one may require some help in coming to a full understanding. For this reason Marion advises: "Ask your parent what they think but if they continue to avoid it they may have good reasons for doing that. You'll just have to accept it." Similarly, Jerry says the decision in such a situation should, and must, lie with the parent: "It's better if parents can be honest, but the mother is the mother and she has to decide how much to tell."

What appears to be the cause of separation may be a distorted view. You may draw your own conclusions from the available facts but you may not have the total picture. Margaret revised her opinion when she saw her mother becoming vengeful and vindictive: "Things might not be what they seem. When my father got home there was nothing for him to return to. Everything was gone, his wife, his children. Everything that reminded him of that life was destroyed. My mom had us all suckered in. She expected my dad just to take it and go. We were all geared up to her story and when he came home she had a court order. She sat there enjoying it. I lost respect for her. I thought, 'What a child.' Suddenly my dad's messing about with other women didn't seem so bad. She seemed childish. I could not forgive him but I lost respect for her even though I know she'll still always be there for me."

The maturity of the child or adolescent seems to be an obvious factor in the parents' decision as to how much of the truth to share. Marion feels "Kids are very impressionable. Tone it down for someone who is 11. Don't express bitterness. But it's better to tell than for kids to see the bitterness and not know why. You're influenced no matter what age you are. The parents should be really careful and make sure they don't say much about it until a person is ready to know."

What comes out of this discussion for me is that parents should make the final decision of when and how much to tell teenagers. But parents are really handicapped in knowing just what level of understanding their teenager might have and how their adolescent son or daughter would respond to certain facts. Parents can only respond if you help them know what you want to hear and how much. If you feel you are mature enough to handle some details, fine, but be very clear with your parent about what you don't want to know. As a general rule it's wise to keep out of your parents' bedroom: discussing details of their sexual life can be very upsetting. Judging by the group of adolescents I spoke with, you may not be able to avoid some sexual material. Approximately one in three adolescents I spoke with gave adultery as the reason for their parents' separation.

No one is perfect. But we often expect more of our parents than of other people. Younger children become very angry with parents who fail to keep a promise or let them down in some way. When we are older we realize that sometimes parents make mistakes, but even though we understand we sometimes feel very angry or disappointed if a parent doesn't live up to the standards that we have set for them. Laurie was very disillusioned when she found out about her father's relationship with another woman: "I found out a lot about my parents through this divorce. Up to the time of the divorce I always thought of my father as God. My feelings toward him were completely shattered. After the divorce I found out he'd fathered a child of one of his best friends' wife. That really sends you. You don't know what to think. At first he ignored us for several months, then he wanted us to go over and visit him. Well, at that time I wouldn't go. I hated this man who had completely destroyed my life, or so I thought. He says he's sorry. He knows he's done a lot of things that he shouldn't have done. It's really hard to put the past out of my mind and accept him for what he is now."

If you are like the group of people I talked with you are likely to have pretty high moral standards for your parents, and these may not be the same moral standards you hold for yourself or your friends. Adultery seems to bring out anger at a parent's deviation from these standards. It's as if a parent broke a special rule. It's not surprising that Annette felt hurt and angry when she learned of her father's girlfriend: "After a couple of weeks after I was told that my parents were getting divorced, I was going up to our boat with my two brothers and my father, and my father was with another lady and this lady used to live just down the street from us when my parents were still married. So it really hurt a lot to think he could do that with another lady while he was still married."

Some people found that, once disillusioned, they quickly began to resent the parent who had had an affair. Richard says, "That's what happened to us. I didn't believe her at first. I felt sorry for my mom 'cause my dad had done this horrible thing to her. I swore I'd never see my dad again 'cause he'd done it." Eventually Richard was able to work out his anger and now is working on getting closer to his father. Marion was not so angry but she did feel sad and hurt. She had asked her dad if he was having an affair and he told her he was: "Their whole romance seemed strange. I thought my dad was making a big mistake when he decided to marry this other lady. But by that time I had written him off. I still love him — I still have terrible pangs of regrets and sorrow from what he did, but I feel that's his choice and I really can't do much about it."

Parents have standards and ethics, perhaps not as strict as people hold when they are adolescent, but they do hold certain values. Sometimes a parent who finds that he or she is unable to live up to these standards experiences a sense of loss and anger at himself or herself. The father who has tried to live up not only to his own moral values but also to the idealized picture his children have of him may feel very guilty about what happened. It may be important to recognize this in your parent and to work through your hurt to come to understand his or her actions. Joel came to understand his father's problems: "As I began to learn things about my father I'd realize that there were a lot of women in his life. That was one realization that I came to which nobody else seemed to be able to figure out. He's had a hard life and he is very disgruntled about what's happened to him. He's an artist and had talent, but because of his own temper and his voicing his own opinions he's kind of become a black sheep. I've talked to his friends. They upset me — they referred to him as screwing around. I didn't seem to have a father. He was a guy I liked but I didn't agree with some of the things he did. A reverend told me to visit him. I found my father and I talked to him. It became quite obvious to me that he did need someone, not just for sexual purposes. In fact, he needs a family to help him. Then I began to visit him regularly." Anger and resentment have a way of backfiring. If you become so angry at your parent because you believe he or she behaved improperly, you may find your parent resenting your anger and accusations. Your parent may tend to withdraw from you.

You may be saying that it's better not to know about adultery. Jeff feels this way. He wishes his father had been able to resist talking about his mother in that way: "About twice a week my father would call us into the living room, my brother and sister and I. He'd tell us to sit down and listen to what he had to say. He'd go on and on, like the whole life story of my mother committing adultery or something like that. All these stories about what happened to her and other men and what a hussy she is and all this stuff. My mother was never like that. She took it from a logical point of view. She never really hid what happened. She'd tell us flat out what happened but never got into things like about him and other women having intercourse or anything like that. You know, kids just don't want to hear any of that: that's between two parents. Nobody wants to hear about their father going out and screwing some other lady when he was still married. That was a hard thing to take, to think that your parents would cheat on one another."

Jeff refers more to the way his father spoke and the amount of detail he insisted on giving them. But Jill feels it's better to know immediately rather than to find out later. Jill says, "I found this paper with this other woman's name on it. I thought he was gay until I found the paper. It made me sympathize more with both my parents. I'd have been happier knowing right away." Marion agrees: "I do resent the adultery. I'm still glad I found out right away, but that might have just been my personality. It sure helped me understand what went on. I appreciated that. I don't like mysteries. It depends if a person is ready. I asked, I was told." It seems that it helps to know about it if one parent has had an extra-marital affair in order to sort out what happened. However, it may be easier to understand that parent's position if you aren't given all the details. Talking to both parents about their feelings for you and their sorrow about what happened may lead to more understanding and respect on both parts.

One other common cause of separation, which seems to require special attention, is the problem of the alcoholic parent. Ted came to the project in order to share his views. He told me that there is not enough information about alcoholism available for teenagers. I want to share with you, in some detail, what Ted told me of what happened in his family. You may be somewhat shocked by what Ted has to say. If you have a parent who is an alcoholic it may help you to feel you are not alone. If not, you may be able to appreciate the difficulties and offer support and understanding to someone who does.

"My father has been an alcoholic for the past 20 years at least. More or less this has played a major role in my life, the life of my family, my brothers and my sister. Through the years, when I was about 6 or so, I knew that my father was an alcoholic. I knew what an alcoholic was and I knew what the problems affiliated with it were. My father was a very violent man. He would take out problems on my mother, like beating her, or myself or my brothers. As the years went on this got to be a very serious problem. My father has been an alcoholic, like I said earlier, for 20 years, but there have been a few major reasons for that. He suffered a brain tumor just after the war so the doctors say that played a major role in his life. His big problem was trying to adapt to society and a sense of trying to go straight. He's just gotten through a period of going it four months without touching a drop of alcohol. Then all of a sudden he goes back to drinking. He said that he just got bored and felt like drinking again. So, because of that, he's started up drinking and he goes through bad habits. He has been in all sorts of institutions and a member of AA. It helped at one time but it just seemed to die off.

"When I was 15 my mother filed for divorce on the grounds of my father being an alcoholic. This upset my father very much. He went on a couple of rampages — very violent rampages. In fact, he tried to strangle my mother to death one time. My oldest brother had to come to the rescue and save her. He is a very violent man when he is drunk but when he's sober he's a super nice guy. He asks us a lot why we don't move back with him and we try and tell him but he doesn't seem to accept it. He has this problem which is hurting all of us, especially himself. One good thing for me is that I don't abuse alcohol. I control myself, mainly because of what I've seen of my father. But these days teenagers abuse alcohol. I see it in my friends and people at school. I'm glad, in a sense, that I went through this experience, because otherwise I might hang around with the wrong people."

A parent who has an alcohol problem is obviously a very troubled person. When sober, he or she can be a most responsible and loving parent. It can be hard to integrate these two parts of one's parent. Dawn says, "When people ask you 'Where's your father?' I just didn't feel like letting them know what kind of person my father was, because to have an alcoholic father makes him seem like a crazy man. In a sense it was true of my father. It was like a split personality, like Dr. Jekyll and Mr. Hyde."

Almost invariably, alcoholism brings with it financial problems for the family. Bev was unaware of her father's alcoholic problem at first, but gradually the family's circumstances made it unavoidable: "I didn't see my dad for about two months because he was living with someone else, one of his friends, and we used to see him every Sunday, and it sort of drifted away down to about every month. I later found out that the reason was my dad was an alcoholic and he never used to pay the bills. My mom was fed up with it so they separated. I didn't have any idea he was an alcoholic. He acted normal to me but every time I went over to his house he had been drinking. He went out West to see if he could get a job because he had been fired from about six previous jobs."

Barbara recalls that as the youngest member of the family she was protected and didn't understand for some time the difficulties with her father's alcoholism. She tried to keep her warm feelings for her father even after everyone else in the family became bitter. Looking back, she can see more clearly what was happening and put it all into perspective: "He didn't come back to the house and then there were some nights when he came to the house and he wasn't allowed in. He was drunk and he was pounding on the door. We weren't allowed to let him in. There was a whole lot of trouble. I couldn't understand why my four brothers hated him. I got mixed up. I got the feeling people hated me. It was hard: I couldn't rely on Mom and I couldn't rely on Dad. It didn't matter to me if Dad was an alcoholic but there were problems and fights. Even if my dad was drunk half the time, he was my dad and I loved him. The boys didn't look at it that way. They were the ones who had to beat Dad up when he tried to hurt Mom. I always heard Mom bragging to other people, 'Oh, I would never do that to my kids. I would never turn them against their father.' Yet it seemed that she got her digs in. When Dad would phone when he was drunk and I hadn't heard from him in a month or two, Mom would say, 'I like how he phones only when he's drunk.' Now that hurts. You don't want to hear about how he only phones you when he's drunk. Oh, there were a lot of bad times. Once Dad got drunk and his problem got worse, we had to sell the house. We moved away but Dad found us by phoning every school in the city and then he watched us go home from the school and found out where we were living. I remember when I was 6, maybe 7, Dad was living with us. He was drunk every night. We weren't getting any sleep. Every night Mom was having to take us five kids and walk up a couple of blocks to a police station. Then the police would go down to our place and pick up my dad and then we'd be able to go back home but by then we'd lost a lot of sleep. That made everybody's nerves bad so we planned to move again, but Dad got out of jail and they talked it over so we lived together again until my parents finally separated when I was 11. After that there were chains on the door to keep Dad out. Dad would get drunk and come and break them and the police would have to come. Then we had to live in public housing 'cause my dad spent all the money. I think this affected me because of our position with money. My father was so unpredictable. He could be sober for three months and then on a binge. It was just no life for my mum. A divorce in our family's case was the best thing that could have been done."

Ted, who has done a lot of serious thinking about this problem, has some advice for other people who are in a similar position to him: "The teachers at school are really informed about alcohol, at least the ones I have this year. In the past few years they have taken special courses in just alcohol which they never learned at university. Now they pass this on to the students. I've learned a few things I never knew about alcoholics even though I've lived with one for most of my life. I wish more of this were taught in the schools for kids who are 10 or maybe even younger. I don't want to be lectured at, but the problems of alcohol should be learned by all people. If you have an alcoholic father encourage your mother to do something. It was more or less of a relief when my parents were finally divorced, for everyone, especially myself because I had problems sleeping. I try to talk to other people whose parents are splitting up because of alcohol. It helps to talk about your experience and know you're not alone. I don't think you should deny it — that's totally wrong."

ADVICE ON "KNOWING WHAT HAPPENED":

For adolescents
1 Ask both your parents if you want to find out something.
2 Try to understand without being too critical — you may not have all the facts.
3 Avoid detailed sexual information.
4 If alcoholism is a problem, read about it, ask some-

one for information or join a group that instructs you in how to help.

For parents
1   Don't attempt to hide the truth.
2   Details are not necessary. Your teenagers appear sophisticated about sexual matters but may be naive about what constitutes mature emotional intimacy.
3   In most communities there are groups for teen-agers who have an alcoholic parent. If alcoholism has been a factor in your separation, help your children get information and assistance about it.

5
Step on a Crack You'll Break Your Mother's Back.

No one really believes that stepping on a crack will break their mother's back. But young children almost do. I can remember as a child running home just to make sure my mother was all right, even though I knew that things in this world don't really happen that way. These kinds of thoughts occur at a time when children strongly believe in magic and their own power to make changes in the world around them just by wishing it so. Little Mary says, "I wish I had a pony," and believes it might come true. But suppose six-year-old Billy, lying in his darkened room, hears his father and mother yelling at each other again. He makes a wish: "I wish Daddy would stop yelling and leave us alone." A week later his daddy does leave and his mummy is crying and says that Daddy's not coming back. Bill believes his wish has come true, and he feels not only sad but guilty. Unreasonable as this may be, even older children sometimes feel responsible and guilty if their parents get divorced.

Guilt

Most adolescents I talked to were very clear in their minds that they were not responsible in any way for their parents' marriage breaking down. But some people did have some guilt feelings in spite of this. Marion describes what happened right after her father said he was leaving: "I went to a park or something and I prayed for my father that he would be forgiven and be happy and that I wouldn't hold any bitterness or anger for him and that my mother would somehow get through all this. But that's what I wanted. You know, it helped but it was so hard to overcome, that feeling of being ripped off, and that feeling of being unloved. I felt sort of thrust out into the cold in the way that my father, you know, thought this lady was more important than his family. And I was lucky also in a way that I wasn't too close to my father and I think — well, that could be an advantage and a disadvantage but it helped me separate myself from him. Like it was more the idea I was separating myself from, if anything, because I knew it wasn't. I just kept saying this to myself. It's not my fault, I had worked for this family so long, helping my sister, helping my mother."

Unlike little Billy, Marion doesn't believe in magical powers or wishes. So how can we understand Marion's sense of guilt even though she knows she wasn't responsible in any way? As well as feeling guilt Marion has two other strong feelings, a sense of being unloved or rejected by her father and a sense of anger and fear of bitterness which might follow this anger. It seems to be a feeling of rejection and anger at the situation that leads to a sense of guilt. Up to about the age of nine or ten children are afraid that if their parents can stop loving each other they can stop loving them. They're afraid their parents will abandon them as they have their husband or wife. As Marion put it, "Little kids don't understand emotion and sex and things. Adolescents know more about people. Obviously guilt is an immediate reaction for a little kid. It's very simple. Adolescents realize more about relationships." Jill says, "The older you are the more perceptive you are. You see it coming."

It seems that young children are so afraid of losing their parents' love that they would rather believe that they caused the divorce. If they are at fault all they have to do is be good and their parents will get back together. Ted notes, "A younger kid wants to patch things up, but an adolescent is more likely to feel anger rather than guilt. I never heard of a case where it's the kids that are to blame."

Asked about their own experience most people said things like: "I don't see any reason to feel guilty. *They* got divorced. I felt no guilt at thirteen. I was not responsible for my parents, and my younger brother and sister didn't feel guilty. They felt sad, not guilty."

Only three people I spoke with had experienced a sense of guilt. When Sharon found out about her parents she felt really guilty: "I was eleven and I thought it was my fault. I kept asking Mom, 'What did I do wrong?' All I could think about was, 'What did I do wrong?' It went away quickly after a few days but at that time I put all the responsibility on me."

While Sharon and Marion had never given their parents any particular trouble Jill felt that she had been difficult to live with and had been involved in her parents' fights: "If I wasn't there, there would have been fewer arguments but the same problems. I'm sure I played a part but not one I feel bad about now." Sally feels that this cannot be seen as the same as feeling responsible for the separation: "Everyone probably feels a little bit guilty depending on the situation, but if a kid was getting into trouble, say, at school he might feel bad."

Similarly Barbara says, "Kids are not guilty. It's between their parents. They'd rather be happy. They don't blame themselves for the break-up. I think if you did you'd need someone strange to talk to. To get out your innermost feelings, you need a stranger." It seems that the best way to deal with confusion about your part in the separation is to talk it out. Ask your parents or speak to someone you trust. Family friends told Bill not to feel guilty and this seemed to be quite helpful. Most parents seem to be really understanding, like Jerry's: "My mother and father, they both felt for me. My mother saw me day to day in my confusion and darkness. They themselves told me I wasn't responsible a couple of times. They sat down separately with me." Likewise, Duncan says of his parents, "They never gave us the thought that we were the problem."

Blame

As an adolescent you will likely neither experience much guilt nor feel much responsibility for the marriage break-up. If you do, it will probably be transitory. But if your parents are separated it's natural to say, "Why me? What have I done?" You will probably feel very angry and you may find yourself putting a lot of energy into establishing who's at fault. It's only human nature to want to blame someone when you're angry. A little child who is just learning to run, when he falls, will turn about and tearfully accuse his mother, "You made me fall down," even though his mother was nowhere near him. Wanting to blame someone, especially a parent, for your misfortune doesn't totally disappear when you mature. I know a forty-year-old man whose mother had been dead ten years. He still feels angry with his departed mother whenever he is in a restaurant and gets a bone in his fish. Even though he knows it doesn't make sense to blame her, he still feels that "my mother should look after me."

You may find yourself looking for someone to blame, someone to be a scapegoat for your anger. One parent or both can become an easy target for your anger. As Nancy suggests, it may help to work it all through: "You put it all together and it sounds like it was my dad's fault. Well it was, but I don't blame him. I guess it just happened, you know." Richard used to blame his father but now seems to understand what happened; it's his father who continues to blame himself. "I don't think my father's ever gotten over this. He thinks we blame him for everything. We don't blame him but he still feels badly."

You may find yourself tending to blame or be angry at one parent rather than the other, particularly if that parent's sexual relationship has been the cause of the separation. Marion's advice on distancing yourself from the situation is sound. Of course, you can't totally deny what's happening or refuse to believe what you know to be the truth, but you can leave fixing of the blame to your parents. Hopefully they, too, will find other ways than blaming to deal with their distress.

Not me, it's him

It's only natural that parents need outlets for their anger too. Blaming can be quite contagious; it spreads rapidly. "My sister is not always nice to my mother. Mom says it's all her own fault for raising her that way. 'What did I do wrong? Oh, that dumb father of yours.' " Nancy feels that her mother is at least partly to blame but she doesn't say so. Instead, she finds kidding her mother out of it works for her. "I just say, 'Sure, sure Mom, it's all your fault.' She doesn't really believe that any more than I do and she just stops."

Interestingly, although most of the people I talked to felt their own behavior was not a major factor in their parents' separations, one in four talked about the involvement of their brothers or sisters. Jerry thinks that, "If someone feels guilty maybe there's a reason — my brother feels that way. He was the main reason they broke up. My mother doesn't say that, my father does. They won't speak to each other. My father won't speak to him anymore."

"I thought it was mostly my older brother's fault," says Richard, "but now I think it's not. He thought he did too because my mother tells him he did. He was just being a scapegoat in the house". Naturally, if someone in the family is in trouble or having problems they can't deal with, it puts a strain on everyone. But I agree with Annette that "if parents started dumping on anyone, they should understand that the parents are blaming them because of their own guilt. Older kids know how to stand up to their parents but even so you might need to go to a counsellor or something."

There are many suggestions on how to deal with parents who blame their children for their misfortune. These range from fighting back to running crying to your room or ignoring them. "When a kid sees the reason for divorce his opinions will be changed." Moreover, Jim advises, "Just ignore them. If they argue, just walk out. I found out two to three years later. The divorce paper had all the reasons of divorce written on it. My brother was responsible mainly, but if a kid is getting into trouble it's up to the parents. A kid has to make the parents see. If they are too blind, go to somebody else, an aunt or an uncle." Jim advises you to ask someone you trust who understands the situation. Also, I would hope that, through understanding that blame may be motivated by feelings of hurt and anger, you might be more able to communicate with your parent. But certainly you can't help anyone, least of all yourself, by becoming involved in blaming other family members. Again, you may find the best solution is to distance yourself from this activity.

Second marriages

Sometimes parents who are badly hurt or feeling rejected enter too quickly into another relationship, either marriage or a common-law union. When there are step-brothers and step-sisters, as well as a new step-parent, in the home this can cause a lot of turmoil as you try to adjust. Often these arrangements break down. A parent who has had a second divorce begins to feel inadequate, very hurt and angry, and is much more likely to get into blaming. If you find yourself in such a situation you may easily become the target for some of the anger and hurt. It is not uncommon to have fights with your step-brothers and step-sisters or step-parent as the situation deteriorates. Jim felt that he played a part in his father's second divorce: "My brother also thinks maybe it was my fault 'cause I didn't get along with the two kids or her. Well they didn't either but, well, I showed more disrespect toward her and I didn't like the kids at all. They were almost the same age as me and I just hated them compared with when I was their age. They were acting so little and immature."

Jeff feels that it is unfair for the parent in this situation to put it on the teenagers: "It may be true but the parent has to be adult and be responsible. They must try to stifle that even if they think it's true. If you thought that two adults had their lives messed because of you it would be really hard." Jerry found it easier to be understanding about his father's second marriage. He says, "Defend yourself. Dad said it was because we didn't get along with her kids and never accepted her. I just have one mother and I don't care how many wives he has — I have just one mother."

Suppose you feel you did behave badly. You can still help your parent without having to accept all the responsibility for this second break-up or without dumping it all back on your parent. Perhaps you could point out how none of you had time to adjust to the first divorce before you all got into a second family situation. Just when you were trying to put a little distance between yourself and all that pain you found yourself right back in it again. Naturally, all your feelings came tumbling out.

This is one situation where you can really assist your parent just by being around. I don't mean that you have to do everything with him, nor do you have to spend long periods of time in deep conversation. But your parent may need reassurance that you intend to stick by him/her.

Loyalty

When you're forced to make choices between one parent and the other this can sometimes make you feel disloyal and guilty. "Choosing to live with one parent encourages guilt feelings about the other parent. It prevents other relationships later on." Jeff adds: "I had strong, strong guilt feelings about moving. Say we wanted to spend Christmas at so-and-so's house. You feel about this high telling the other parent you can't be there. It's just like a referee in a hockey game. One side's happy, one side's mad. I saw a show once on the 'Children of Divorce'. It said they were like pawns in a chess game — always moved around but they never win."

When her mother looks depressed, Abby feels guilty: "I still feel that I should be responsible for my mother, and if she's feeling bad about something I feel guilty and it shouldn't be that way, I guess, because she's responsible for herself. But somewhere in between that I saw my mother getting hurt a lot of times by my father and I still see her getting hurt and she's a very strong person now, but I just feel badly. I feel that I wish I could do more to help her a lot of the times, and I think that what other kids have to realize is that they're just in the middle of it and that's separation or divorce — it doesn't seem to happen because of them."

Even people whose parents are not separated sometimes feel a strong pull towards one parent or the other. You are more likely to feel this kind of guilt if you think your parent will be angry or resent your behavior. For example, if your father invites you to go on a trip with him and your mother hasn't had a real holiday in over a year, you're likely to feel guilty about going. You imagine your mother will be hurt and angry that you're having a good time while she's left behind. But you have to check it out. Although she may be sorry that she isn't getting a vacation, this doesn't mean she doesn't want you to have one. She is definitely not resenting you for being happy. You may still feel badly for her but your guilt feelings will probably diminish.

Some people experienced guilt when they heard one parent degrading the other parent. They felt that they were being disloyal to the other parent by listening. Margaret says, "I don't know the reason why, but I felt guilty that I have to be there when Mom goes off on her money bit. I feel guilty that I'm one of the ones she's been bugging for eighteen years." Margaret also felt that, "Even if you love someone like your mother, you can't take their problems onto yourself. It just tears you right apart. I feel that if my parents hadn't, if my mother hadn't told me about the situation that was going on, I would have been far better off. There were guilt feelings that I was loving one more than the other even though I didn't think I was." She goes on to describe how she handled this: "I told Mom off if she knows she's making me feel guilty by flying off the handle and that I'm going to walk away." I can't totally agree with Margaret here. Her mother is not *making* her feel guilty. Everyone is responsible for their own feelings. Margaret's mother is expressing anger and bitterness: she is not trying to make Margaret feel guilty. Her mother may not be aware of what Margaret is feeling, so it is important that Margaret let her mother know that she feels guilty and disloyal if she listens.

Feeling unwanted

Like Margaret's mother, parents sometimes say things that they do not intend to be taken literally. Laurie feels guilty "in a way because sometimes my parents would say, 'If we could do it all over again there would be no kids.' It was a kind of feeling of rejection. When it boils right down to it, I don't think we had anything to do with it." Feeling this sense of rejection can set a person up for self-blame and guilt.

A person can become obsessed with fear of rejection and worry about it as Gordon has: "I don't believe it for an instant that my parents, especially my mother in going out West to live, rejected me but I still have that feeling with me. It still exists. I still think maybe there's a remote chance she did reject me. I can't totally shut my brain waves off to that. Same with my father. He's a good provider but a bit indifferent. He never shows any kind of restriction or disapproval. My parents just seemed to let me do whatever I wanted. It seemed to be a bit of indifference but I'm not sure. But I'm still plagued by the fact that they rejected me."

When they're very tired or frustrated, all parents have the momentary wish to be free of responsibility for children. Even older teenagers can seem a heavy burden. You may be able to see that statements made at such times are expressions of their frustrations and not a true desire to abandon you. Such is the case with Elizabeth: "My sister and I are not responsible: we have no guilt. Of course, it would be easier if we weren't born but my parents both explained that they had us at a time when we were very much wanted and loved. Out of love they had us, so we never felt guilty."

More blame

Some people in the group found that they were being blamed for some of the trouble by people outside their immediate family. "My grandmother blamed me," recalls Barry. "My father is an only child. My grandmother came down on me for breaking it up. She always hated my mother." Jennifer found that her friends kept asking her if it was her fault that her parents split up. Barbara had an unusual experience: "My aunt came down on me for keeping them together for so long." Ted reinforces the position that children are responsible neither for breaking up a marriage nor for keeping it together: "Most cases I've seen myself personally, none of the kids have ever been the reason why their parents split up. It's mainly due to the fact that it has been dragging on for years and years like it did with my parents."

Working it through

In summary then, a situation where feelings of guilt or blame are involved is best dealt with by talking it out, usually with your parents, but, if that's not possible, with a close understanding relative. A friend who has gone through the same experience may guide you. This seems, however, to be one of the very few situations where it may not be wise to talk with friends whose parents have not separated: they may not fully understand.

Barry, who describes his own working through of his feelings of anger and guilt, might be the best one to have the last word on this subject: "After, I felt so close to my mother and my sisters. I guess you have to be to survive. Talking about it with them got your feelings out in the open and made you realize that you weren't at fault. That was one problem I had. I thought I was at fault with a lot of it, and all it really needs is people to tell you right afterwards that it had nothing to do with you. You're somebody completely separate. I guess after the major crisis was over and everybody had sort of settled down, we'd — my sisters and I and my mother — we'd sit down at the dinner table or something and discuss different feelings we had about our father — not compare notes, just discuss feelings. I guess we decided then what we thought of him and different things like that. I guess the whole separation was due to my father. Unfortunately, well fortunately, I guess, both my parents, it wasn't just him. When our family is sitting around discussing the good and bad things he's done, we begin to fit it together and piece it together and decide where it started and different things. Where he even had a girlfriend before this one or what. You know what exactly happened that's interesting. That also reassures you that you're not to blame because, as I said before, this was a big problem at the beginning. I felt really responsible for the separation and all it needed was for someone to tell me that that was stupid. But I think getting your aggressions out is the main thing. However you do it is your own choice but if you leave them in, not only will they build up something bad but also it's more destructive inside. It's more destructive on yourself if you let things sit."

ADVICE:

For adolescents
1 Express anger at the situation, express hurt — avoid blame. For example: "I feel really angry and unloved when I see Mom with her boyfriend," as opposed to, "The whole thing is Mom's fault for getting involved with that man."
2 Ask questions and reason things out.
3 Talk to someone: your parents, your friends, family friends or a counsellor.

For parents
1 Express anger, hurt, but don't apportion blame.
2 Reassure your kids they're not to blame even if they say they know that.
3 If your child's been in trouble, redirect your anger at your ex-partner for lack of support in helping your son or daughter. Don't blame the child.
4 It's natural and normal, at times, to feel that you want to be rid of your kids. Make sure they understand the difference between this momentary wish and a lack of love or abandonment of them.

6
Who's Coming With Me?

The question of custody can be one of the most distressing issues in a separation or divorce. If both your parents are reasonable and can come to an agreement about who you should live with, then you may not experience the intense conflict of loyalties that such a question brings. Once parents begin legal action, feelings are very intense and usually hostile. This is enhanced by the adversary system, by which I mean that each parent's lawyer tries to act as well as he can for his own client. Under the law you will probably not be recognized as a party in a divorce action. This means that only the husband and wife in the situation are seen as having business before the court and so only their lawyers are routinely recognized to represent them. This may seem grossly unfair to you as you are one of the persons most directly affected by the separation. You probably didn't want the separation, and may feel as if you're being "batted around like a ping pong ball" without your feelings, or indeed your rights, being considered by the law.

Jerry talks at length about what it was like for him to be involved in a custody battle: "My dad came and told us they were getting a divorce. My father went downstairs and I asked my brothers if my parents get divorced where would they go. Who will they stay with? I told them I was staying with my father no matter what and my little brother, he follows me quite often, he said the same thing. My second oldest brother said he was going with my mom, as was my oldest brother. Nothing happened for a few days. Then we went to my grandparents' house to return something we'd borrowed. My father came into the house and words were exchanged because my grandparents had known that my mom was going to divorce him. They didn't care too much for my father. There was a fight — not a big fight, just a small little scuffle in the living-room with my mother's brother and my father. A lot of action took place in a short amount of time. A lot of screaming, hysteria from my mother's side of the family. My eldest brother, Jack, was there at the house when this happened and so were my other two brothers as well as myself. This is when it became time to ac- tually choose who we were going to stay with or live with for the time being. My father eventually was ready to leave the house and he said, 'Who's coming with me?' and I said 'I am', and my little brother said, 'I'm coming with you.' That's to follow me again, I guess. He said to my second oldest brother, 'Come on', and my brother said, 'No, I'm not coming.' My dad told my mother, well, he had asked my mother first, 'Come on, we're leaving.' She said that she was staying. So my father took myself and my little brother and we got in the car and we went home. My mother, second oldest brother, my oldest brother, they stayed at my grand- parents' house. I think the hardest point in the whole thing was that little yo-yo routine there at my grand-parents'. When my father actually said, 'Who's coming with me?' and I said I was — my mother, at the same time as I went to my father, my mother grabbed at one arm and my father grabbed at my other arm and it was like a tug of war. They were actually pulling me. Each one wanted me. I was like, I was sort of an object that they had to have. I guess they both loved me, and both wanted me, but just for some reason I had to go with my father. I really don't know why.

"My father, when I was smaller, was always the one who, you know, would carry out the discipline. My mother was always, you know, nice about it, about things. She'd give what I wanted more than my father would, but at a time like that I guess you just have to choose and I think I made the right decision. I think for anybody else who would have to go through a time like that, if they had to actually choose who they would want to go with, if they were at that age, you know, where they could make the choice — I think it's very difficult to have to sit down in front of them with no, you know, nothing like what happened at my grand-parents' house, and have to say I want to go with you or you, you know. The position I was in, I had to make a choice right away and I knew I had to make the right choice and I did. I think I was quite mature for my age (13). If another person will have to do the same thing, well, I really can't give any advice for that. It would be something, it would have to be, you know, their own choice, and it would have to be what they actually thought deep down inside was really best for them.

"When I got home, my father and my brother, we were real quiet. We were crying and quite scared. My father had his finger broken during the fight and he was in a real bit of pain. After a while a policeman drove up because my grandmother had called the police. He wanted to know what had happened and, well, he left after a couple of minutes. There was nothing much happening. As I spoke to my father a little later on I found out that he wasn't going to grant a divorce to my mother. He said that he would fight it. Well, this was after he was served by the sheriff's office with the, I guess, petition for the divorce. He said, well, after he was served with the petition the grounds were physical and mental cruelty. He definitely did not want to — well, if she should win the divorce he felt that that means he was guilty of the crime or the grounds and he said that he wasn't guilty. If she wanted a separation that was fine. He didn't want to pay any alimony. That was another reason I guess for wanting to fight it.

"Time went on and my father got a lawyer, my mother had a lawyer. I hadn't spoke to my mother maybe three or four weeks and I remember she called us up and she wanted to talk — well, she wanted to at first and from that conversation she started calling every day, speaking to us. I didn't mind speaking to her at that point. I didn't think it was really — I didn't have any hate towards her so I spoke to her. Eventually, we went out and I went over to visit her. She got set up in an apartment and in the apartment she had bought she had three rooms, one room for herself, one room for my older two brothers and she said she had the other room for myself and my little brother. I told her that I'm not coming to live with her but she said that I was, that she was going to get me and I had to go and live with her. This is when I started to, you know, started to feel some kind of hate towards her because she's so stubborn that she wouldn't let me choose who I wanted to live with or how I wanted to live. She said I must live with her. In the court she not only filed for divorce she also wanted custody of myself and my younger brother, as well as she wanted a number of other things, the house, as much money as she could get, also.

"It took quite a while until the case came up. There was a lot of preliminary hearings and things like that, that I wasn't involved in but my father had made copies of all the manuscripts and things like that and they were available to me any time I wanted to read them and I did read them and I understood them and there was a number of things in there that I didn't — that were wrong. That my mother had testified to, made up things — in my mind anyways — and this just added. I started more and more, started to hate my mother and eventually I started having fights with her and until one point where I just wouldn't speak to her but my little brother, he maintained that, you know, conversation with her and he went and visited her. It was getting closer now to the trial date and there's going to be a trial and I was supposed to go down.

"My father asked me if I wished to testify and I said I would and my younger brother said he would. Speaking to my older two brothers they had said that they were going to go down too and testify. Just before the court appearance the judge had ordered that the whole family go down for, I think it was psychiatric treatment. I thought, 'There's no way I'm going to see a psychiatrist. I'm not crazy and I don't need to.' This really made me feel a lot of anger towards my mother because it was her doing by wanting to try to get me and my smaller brother and with the whole divorce and things — it was her fault that we had to go through all these — we had to go through this examination. I also had a social worker come to the house and she took us away for a little while, a couple of days, three days, and I didn't want to go through all this. I just wanted to be left alone and I was constantly being pressured by all these people. I thought that to my choice I wanted to live with my father why don't they leave me alone, but my mother still maintained that she had to have me.

"Finally, we went to court. My mother's lawyer succeeded in having myself, my youngest brother banned from the courtroom because we were too young to testify. Some legal way of getting us out. But the judge asked us to come into his chambers and wanted to talk to us. Just myself and my younger brother. He took us in, I remember he asked me what would happen if he would award myself to my mother and my little brother to my mother and I told him that I wouldn't go. He said I would be breaking the law. I said, 'Well, I'd break the law then. I wouldn't stay with her.' If I was forced to I'd run away and there's no way I was going to live with her. He asked me why. I don't even know if I gave a reason. I just said that 'I'm not going to.' Well, we went back into the court and I think it was that same day that he made a decision on custody and he awarded myself and my brother to live with my father.

"I think he did say he was going to award us to my mother but after speaking with us he changed his mind. That's when my mother, well, she felt really bad but, well, after that she found out that she had won a divorce and she had won a number of other things, a large amount of money, etc. I think after that she was quite happy. She moved from that apartment to a smaller apartment because she didn't need a big one now and life sort of went on for me. I started speaking to her again. I went to visit her maybe once a week, on a Sunday. I spoke to her on the 'phone a couple of times a week. I would never call her. She'd always call me."

Not everyone has an experience like Jerry's of such open conflict. Many people say that there was no question as to where they would live: it was obvious. When one parent moves out, it makes sense to remain

in your own home, in your same school and neigh-
bourhood. Most custody decisions favor the mother: in
our group, mothers had custody in five out of every
seven cases.

If your parents want a divorce, they have to go
through a court procedure. After the divorce is granted,
the judge decides on the issue of custody as well as
visitation rights, alimony and child support. The time
it takes to actually get to the divorce court varies in
different places in the country. But as you are aware
the decision who you will live with at least temporarily
must be made at the time of the separation. In the
group I spoke with most people were happy, or at least
content with the solution arrived at in their own circumstances. Michael says, "I wanted to be with my
mother and this was what it was. I couldn't live with
my father. I know that would hurt me." If your parents
don't divorce within the first year to eighteen months
they are not likely to divorce, if the group is an in-
dication, until three to six years later. Jeff says of his
parents, "They fought so long that by the time the
decision came around we were over 16.

"Eighty percent of the group stayed with the
parent they first lived with after separation. Harold
and Karen are two of the exceptions.

Karen's parents have joint custody which, in her
case, means she lives six months with her mother and
then six months with her father. She likes the
arrangement except that, "Six months is too short a
time. I'd rather live longer in one place. There's too
much moving." Joint custody means that both parents
are the responsible guardians for their child's welfare.
While some parents take this to mean that their child
should live half the time with one parent and half the
time with the other, all kinds of arrangements are
made. Some joint custody arrangements are that the

child lives all the time with one parent but both parents work together on decisions that have to be made. Other arrangements are flexible with the child or teenager staying at whichever household is more convenient. Still others are very rigid so that the child lives three days with one parent and four days with the other. I have not heard of any that have more frequent changes than this last type. When I asked the group what they thought of the notion of parents each having equal time, as a way of resolving the conflicts about custody, I got some pretty negative answers.

Jim says, "The sex of the parents makes a big difference. You hear of these precedents where you get to stay one year with one parent. This is not good." Others said that they'd feel like a yo-yo, or unwanted. Annette was concerned that she might not want to return after six months: "If I wanted to go one way my parent would be angry at the other parent and say, 'You've turned her against me.'"

Harold first lived with his father when his mother moved out. Later, his father went to live with a girlfriend so his mother moved back in. But he couldn't get along with his mother so he went to his father's new home. When his father broke up with his girlfriend, Harold went back to his mother's. Now he's with his father, his father's new girlfriend and her three children. To add to the confusion, Harold has an older brother and sister who were moved around almost as much as he was.

What about splitting up brothers and sisters? Some people have suggested boys should go with their fathers and girls with their mothers. Duncan recalls, "It was just awful. My mother wanted me to put my brother and my father right out of my life. But he (my brother) kept in touch with me and finally, at one point, he said, 'I finally realize what Dad's done and how much it hurts the whole family.' He said that he wanted to come home. That was really a turning point. I was so happy that he wanted to come back and I brought it up with Mom. It was really a rough scene. She wanted nothing to do with him." Abby and Bev agree that "Kids should stay together if possible." As John says, "With kids it's more important to stay together. But even at 13 or 14 there is a lot of dependency on each other, when you can't depend on your parents." When you lose a parent it is painful enough without also losing daily contact with your brothers and sisters. As a general rule as little change as possible should occur in the first period after a separation. If you do find that your living arrangements are such that you are separated from a brother or sister, try to keep in touch as much as possible. Not only may you find their support welcome, but they may need you just as badly as you need them.

In most cases, then, custody is decided long before couples go to court. A study done in England showed that 98% of couples who come before the divorce court had agreed previously who should have custody. In some parts of the United States, the courts hold informal meetings at which the judge, or someone appointed by the judge, and the parents try to resolve custody and other issues before they appear in the formal courtroom. But most parents agree about custody and leave it at that without a legal battle.

Many parents choose to put their agreements about custody in writing with the help of a lawyer. This is what is known as a separation agreement and is what people usually mean when they talk about a legal separation. A separation agreement records what the parents have decided about custody and how they have decided to divide their property and income. It is a legal document in the sense that one parent can get the court's help to enforce the agreement if the other parent does not live up to it. You will probably not be directly involved in the preparation of this agreement but may wish to ask both parents' permission to know what it says.

When parents finally appear before the divorce court, the judge will usually agree with what they have decided in their separation agreement. However, a situation can change and what was a good decision a year before might not be the best arrangement at the present time. It's important to remember that the custody arrangement in the separation agreement can be changed if a parent feels that the circumstances have altered sufficiently to warrant it. Either parent can ask the judge to change the custody arrangement.

All these legalities can be confusing. What applies to one person's situation may not apply to another person's. Don't assume that your experience will be identical to those of your friends who have been through a parental divorce. I suggest you ask your parents to explain what they understand to be happening. If this isn't sufficient perhaps you can write your questions down and your father or mother can get the answers from his or her lawyer.

Suppose your parents have just separated but nothing is definitely settled. You may find that both parents want you to live with them and that they try to "entice" you away from the other parent. This was a real problem for Sally, who was living with her mother: "My father, within a year, began telling my brother that if we came to live with him all the fantastic things we would have. Everything we'd always wanted he would give us. All he wanted was someone to live with and we didn't realize this. My father got very angry and started not paying the monthly cheque to my mother for a sum of money that had been in the agreement. There was a lot of negative feelings toward our whole family. My mother couldn't tell us at our age — my brother was 14 and I was 12 — that our father was a liar and all he wanted was someone to live with. He didn't really want us kids. My father found a person to live with who had two little boys. So he moved back into the house which we have lived in before and completely forgot about us moving in with him. My brother and I felt we weren't wanted by my father anymore after all the stuff he'd proposed to give us the year before." Sally's experience raises two questions. Should adolescents be asked whom they want to live with, and at what age would someone be capable of understanding enough to make a good decision?

First, let's talk about how much say an adolescent should have in the final decision. Michael feels strongly that Sally's dad acted improperly: "I don't think it's right for parents to try to influence the child away from the other parent because it tears at the kid. I loved both my mother and my father. I didn't want to set one against the other. Adolescents should have a major say. Happiness depends in part on who he wants to live with. If both parents want custody the adolescent should have a large say." The people I asked varied in their thinking as to how much weight an adolescent's wishes should carry. But everyone felt adolescents should be heard, or at least be given a choice to give his or her opinion. However, only one in four felt that the decision should be totally left up to the teenager. Other concerns which came up were whether you have all the facts, how you would tell one parent you didn't want to live with him or her and then ask to visit the next week, and when you should be asked to make a choice: should you be asked before any other considerations are weighed, or only if both parents can provide equally?

What was the experience of the people in the group with questions of custody? Fifty percent of the adolescents I asked about this said that they were not consulted, and most didn't want to be. Eighteen percent said it was obvious who would have custody; and 30% said they weren't asked. Jeff recalls, "We all sat around the kitchen table. My father had gone out to find his lawyer. My mother told my brother and I that they had decided to split and it was our choice where we wanted to live. That was the biggest thing — who should go where. They left everything up to us. My little brother was supposed to come and live with my mother but I didn't think it would be very good for him because there was just no way that two out of three of us could come and live with my mother without my old man absolutely freaking because my brother and sister are very close and there is just no way you could split them up. So if my brother came that means my sister would probably come which would leave just my father and myself. I decided I should come and live with Mother. It's not really, really good. She goes out of town quite often. When my brother told my mother that he would not be coming to live with her she started crying and all that so I decided one of us would have to go and thought it would be me, as my brother and sister just wouldn't separate. Up until that point it had always been the three of us. Just the three of us going where we want but I thought it would only be fair to my mother to have one of her children for a certain amount of time. Up to the time when we were trying to decide who we were going to live with, our parents would always ask us flat out. It's a really hard thing to tell the parent that you're not going to live with them after you've spent your entire life and gone through so many things together, just to say 'Sorry, I'm leaving.' They take it personally. My father's never really been the same to me since the day I moved out. I would still say that's the hardest part of it."

Putting the whole weight of the decision on a child, even on an adolescent, seems to be very unfair. Perhaps since this decision involves the whole family it should be discussed by everyone on neutral ground. Harold's family went to a counsellor: "We decided where I would go. You could call Legal Aid and get details but you really need a counsellor as well." If Barbara had been forced to make her own decision she might have regretted it. She says, "Make sure you've got your head on straight before you know where you're going. I had so much hate for my mother I would have gone with my father but he was an alcoholic and that would have been trouble."

Now to the second issue, the age at which someone is competent to make their own decisions. Thirteen to fourteen years was mentioned most often by the group as the age at which an adolescent would be competent to make a choice. The group made a clear distinction between being asked your opinion and making the final decision. As Margaret puts it, "This depends on the intellectual development and self-concept and knowing what the fight has been about. If you are able to speak for yourself and are old enough to make little decisions then talk about it with your parents. But after 14 you can make your own decisions. You may need more information. Younger kids don't understand sexuality, that's where growing up sexually comes into it, and your emotions. Definitely under 11 you couldn't know, but you should be consulted." Some people were concerned that younger children would choose the parent who tended to spoil them. Jill says, "At 13 a person is capable of rational thought. They'd work it out, not necessarily go for treats. It's difficult even then. How does a person of 13 raise the question of emotional cruelty?''

So what can we make of these comments? It seems that if you are like the majority of the group you will want to be heard, you will want your feelings to count — but you may not want to be actually forced into making the final decision. Don't feel you have to: if your parents can't decide, you may need outside help.

A family friend, a counsellor or a lawyer might help you to communicate your wishes to your parents. The law is set up to protect you from having to be your parents' judge and jury. You might want to say, "I think it would be better for me to go with Mother for these reasons. On the other hand it would be good for me to go with Dad for these reasons. However, I don't want to make the final decision. That's up to you."

Suppose your parents can't decide reasonably about custody. There may be a custody hearing in court. Should you be involved at this point? Only two people of all those I talked with had been to court and neither was allowed into the actual courtroom. Both Jim and Jerry saw a judge in his office. Laurie has very unpleasant memories of even a peripheral involvement with the courts: "Court was pretty bad in itself. The first time we went to court, I was the only one who had proof about my father committing adultery. He went into a sad story about how he couldn't afford to pay money and all this stuff and her (my mother's) lawyer would not bring me into the courtroom to say that I had seen he was committing adultery. The judge was really good but he didn't know what was happening.''

It seems hard at first to understand why adolescents should be excluded from the courtroom, especially when they have something to contribute.

This is done to protect you. What might look like distortion or lying when you read the transcript is not necessarily what it appears to be. Lawyers are bound to present their client in the best possible way to the court. The court procedure is deliberately set up to look at facts rather than feelings. Judges and lawyers try to keep children and adolescents out of the courtroom in order to protect their feelings.

Even though you aren't present at the actual proceedings you may be offered a secondhand look. Many parents of adolescents offer to let them read the transcripts of the proceedings. Since divorce court proceedings are public, anyone can purchase the record (this is not like some family courts where the records are kept private to protect the children). I question the motives of parents who want their children to read the transcripts of the court hearing. I fear that the parent may be very angry at what has happened in court and is seeking revenge by turning the child against the other parent. If your mother or father offers to let you read these documents you might save yourself some pain by refusing. Or you might ask why he or she wants you to read them. Then, you can judge how much you want to listen to or whether you can help your parent with his or her anger. If you decide to read the papers, try to keep in mind that the court is set up to deal with legal matters to decide whether or not divorce should be granted — not to establish who's at fault. Therefore, whole areas that you think are important may be totally overlooked.

Harold discovered how painful it could be to read the court report and the possible repercussions. "I wish I could have gone to court. My mother purchased the court records. I was living with my mother and everything was okay. We were getting along well. Then one week I found out that my father had bought a townhouse. Well, he split the ownership with his girlfriend for her daughters and my brother to live in. When my mother took my father to court, he got away very lucky and only had to pay very minimal support but he said he was buying a townhouse for his 3 children to live in. Huh! He's full of shit! Then it turns out that he's bought the townhouse for himself and his girlfriend, her two daughters and my brother. When I came over and asked him why I wasn't included in his plans he just said, 'If you wanted a place to stay you would have said something.' That's my father's way of getting out of telling the truth." So adolescents are not likely to be invited into court, not given the present climate of the judiciary.

If you do go to court you will probably see the judge alone in his office as Jim and Jerry did. The judge may ask you where you want to live. If he does he's asking for your opinion, he is not asking you to make the decision for him. Since you won't know what has gone on in court it is important that you explain your reasoning to the judge. He must decide how much weight to give your opinion, and he can't do that without knowing that you're competent. Judges try their best to understand and to act on your interest, but they can't read minds. Seeing the judge privately is a kind of protection for you: if you tell him your views he will probably not report this back in court — but he may. What you say to him may well be reported to your parents. Jim was angry because he wanted the judge to tell everyone what he said. Barbara feels that, although the judge's role is a difficult one, he must bear the responsibility of the decision: "The judge should help a kid get their head straightened out. It's copping out to give one year to one parent. The judge must take all the responsibility. He should take all situations on his shoulders. He should listen to everyone. The judge should base his decision on: 1) Where the kid wants to go. 2) Who's going to be better for him. 3) Age must be judged on emotional stability."

Some community groups are advocating that children have the right to be involved and even to have an equal share in the proceedings. They want children recognized as a "party" in the divorce action. I asked the group whether they thought adolescents should be involved in the court. Most people felt they didn't want to go into the court itself, but they did want a chance to express their opinions somehow. Jill was concerned that if she went to court one or both of her parents might turn against her: "Court brings out bitterness. My parents haven't seen each other once since the divorce in court." Suggestions as to how adolescents or younger children might be involved included having them fill out questionnaires that could be evaluated, or talking to a court-appointed person in privacy or having their own lawyer. Richard advocates a special person: "Kids should be talked to routinely and given a booklet to read. The court offers protection to the child from the parents buying him off. I think kids should be involved in any custody thing, not just divorce. It's too late by the time of divorce. Everyone is settled in."

Some of the adolescents in the group felt that all kids should be interviewed by a special person, "not a judge, as he might be prejudiced." Duncan goes on to say, "A judge can't really know about parents. But I'd always resent the person who helped me choose. It should be an independent person who says what's best."

Others felt that this person should be one who has more training in helping people make up their minds. Bob feels a counsellor is not always necessary, but in the case of contested custody one could help. "A kid should have a lot of say. If parents couldn't discuss it — at this point the parents are probably irrational — then you should find a social worker. He could find out what the kid really wants and who he wants to live with. He should find someone with whom he's really comfortable." If, at any point, you feel you want to talk to a counsellor, you can ask your parent if they would help you find one. If you are concerned your parent might worry, you could arrange to go yourself to a counsellor, bearing in mind that you may need your parent's written permission to attend. This need for your parent's consent usually applies up to the age of 16-18 in some areas of the country, even older in others. Most communities now have social and community information centres you can call for advice on how to obtain a counsellor.

Suppose you're not happy with the custody arrangements. When I asked the group the question "Can custody be changed?", only two people knew that a custody order can be questioned or appealed. How is this done? First you have to have a valid reason for seeking change. Second, an appeal or re-opening requires the assistance of a lawyer. Either parent can make the request through his or her own lawyer or you may want to obtain your own lawyer. How do you know if you need a lawyer? It's important to remember that lawyers do two things. They go to court and represent their clients or take some action on their behalf. But the most important task of a lawyer is to offer advice. Dawn has her own lawyer: "I have a lawyer. It's really helpful. He explains everything. My father arranged it for me." Ted feels, "A lawyer shouldn't know the parents, so a kid can trust him. It's important so the parents won't know what he says. But the lawyer should tell him if it's going to come out in court. A kid needs proper representation. I think a younger lawyer would be better. I would be more open."

Sally asks, "But doesn't the lawyer tell the parents what you say?" This issue of confidentiality or privileged communication with a lawyer is a delicate one where children and adolescents are concerned. Most lawyers feel that a "minor" who is "competent" is able to expect confidentiality and can "instruct" the lawyer. This means that unless you tell the lawyer to do so he can't act on your behalf and he can't reveal what you've told him.* If he feels you aren't competent, however, he will do what he thinks is best for you or in your "best interest". What a lawyer *must* do is explain his policy to you before you start. You can find out the names of two or three lawyers who deal with family law by calling the Bar Association or asking a good lawyer. There is one other safeguard. You are free to "retain" or go to whatever lawyer you want. Remember that just as he is free to withdraw from the case, so you are equally free to discharge him if you aren't satisfied. After all, you are paying for his services.

How do you pay a lawyer? Assuming that you have no funds of your own, you can apply for funds through Legal Aid or the Public Defender's Program. You may get some initial opposition when you tell them why you want a lawyer. Legal Aid is usually very prepared to provide funds for minors for criminal matters but much less willing to do so in civil cases. Divorce, of course, is a civil matter. But you must be persistent. Sometimes it's possible to get a loan from Legal Aid which you pay back later when you've finished school and are working.

But a word of caution before you engage a lawyer. Gordon says, "O.K., so you can get a lawyer, but are you even ready to talk to a lawyer? If they changed the legislation you could conceive of a kid battling against

* I'm saying "he" for the sake of convenience but, of course, you might choose a woman lawyer.

the court." Perhaps you don't need your very own lawyer if all you need is advice and explanation. "I think it's good to have a lawyer," says Jerry. "My father's lawyer explained things to me and went to court. You don't really need a third lawyer." One of the best reasons I've heard of for having a lawyer was John's. "It might serve to keep a kid out of court. A kid wouldn't have to come because he would have a representative there."

You may simply want advice from a lawyer on the laws in your State. For example, the age at which you are entitled to leave home or make your own decision about where you want to live may be lower than the age of majority in your State. You might get this kind of information about the law from the Department of the Attorney General or the public library without having to engage a lawyer.

Unfortunately, in post-divorce cases "maintenance" or money paid to the custodial parent for support of the children is argued over much more than which parent should have custody. Most adolescents said that their parents abided by the court decision about custody and visiting but alimony was quite a different matter. "I still feel the alimony payments are harder to deal with for kids because my father would always bring up things. He would tell us how much he pays my mother and I started to feel guilty about how much he pays. I guess it's frustrating for him because he does pay us a lot more than he has to and we don't know what it is we buy with it." Sally's experience is much the same: "He still and always felt that the money he paid each month for my brother's and my care was actually going to my mother for her entertainment. This is obviously not true. My brother and I have tried to persuade him but we're not very successful. Just now both of us are reaching the point that we can stand up to him but the years before we've been scared of him and he couldn't see that he was hurting us. He continued to pay the alimony whenever he felt he wanted to. This got my mother upset."

Most people felt that it was fair that the non-custodial parent should pay something, like Bill's father: "He pays — I don't know how much. It's right that he should." Annette says, "I'm not sure how much it is. It's a certain amount at the beginning of the month. He doesn't pay at all. She just doesn't get paid. Mom doesn't have much money right now. I'm scared of my Dad but if Mom doesn't take it to court I'll speak to him." Some people found themselves getting involved and angry. "My father refuses to give alimony," says Ted. "He's absolved himself from all duties. I wouldn't be able to 'phone him up and borrow money even for the dentist's bill."

But some teenagers were just as angry and embarrassed because their custodial parents were asking for too much. Margaret is embarrassed by the situation: "It's sort of cheap. I feel I'm being used to get back at him. It bothers me. I don't think he should pay for her anyway. If I were a male, I wouldn't pay. She should get a job and look after herself." It can be very frustrating, according to Jeff, to have to deal with parents' continuing legal entanglements over financial arrangements: "My parents never stopped fighting. It's still going on now. I'm really frustrated when I hear them talking about some of their blues. They're both making a good buck but they're both putting a lot of money each year to lawyers. We've heard it all before. We really don't want to hear it again. But they air their legal hassles. At the moment they're hassling over my father's farm which he purchased when my parents were married and now my mother wants some large amount of money out of it because she thinks she should have it as she lived with him so long."

Although it is probably good advice for adolescents to stay away from the financial issues as much as possible, there are some instances where you might want to become involved. For example, Michael was concerned, "The support payments only go until your 18. But I want to go to university. So then there won't be sufficient money. I've some other problems. My father held back a number of times because he didn't see enough of us. Eventually he went to court and now we see him more regularly." This is a special area of the law that deals with the parents' responsibilities to their children, even though those children may have reached an age when normally they would be self-sufficient. In some States Michael might be entitled to go to court to ask for a continuance of his maintenance in order to complete his college education. If this applies you might want to seek advice either through your parents' lawyer or through your own lawyer.

Wherever possible with financial matters, let the lawyers and the courts decide what's right and fair. This helps you to avoid feelings of being bought off by a parent or having one parent feel you're siding with the other.

ADVICE ON CUSTODY AND MAINTENANCE:

For adolescents
1 Don't get involved in the legal matters unless you have to. Especially avoid financial arrangements.
2 Get all the information you need before making a decision. Seek the *advice* of a lawyer, if necessary.
3 Don't answer the question, "Who's going with me?", if you can avoid it. Ask to speak with someone outside the family whom you trust.
4 Do give your opinions, both the pros and cons. Ask

to see your parents' or your own lawyer about areas of direct concern to you, like custody and visiting. Be sure to instruct your lawyer what you want to remain confidential.

For parents

1   Your adolescents don't want the responsibility of making the decision about custody. But they *do* want to be heard.

2   Protect your kids from all the legal battles. Tell somebody else.

3   Do answer all the questions they have and if they want, arrange for them to meet with your lawyer. Don't be hurt if your son or daughter seeks private counsel.

4   The law takes seriously the entitlements of a child to support. Make sure your child receives the maintenance to which he or she is entitled. But be wary — teenagers rapidly lose respect for a parent who abuses this by demanding excessive maintenance.

5   Further splitting of the family is not usually a good idea. Try to keep the children together as a unit for mutual support.

7
Did Your Father Say Anything About Me?

Living with one parent brings up the question of visiting the absent parent. If you are like most adolescents you will want to visit with your parent fairly regularly. The arrangements you make will depend, in part, on how far you live away from your parent (or parents if you live alone). Some people go once a year for an extended visit while others have a more casual arrangement of "drop in any time". Seven out of ten of the teenagers I talked to live with their mothers, and most of these live in the same city as their fathers. Karen's parents have decided on joint custody; so visiting is very regular and quite strict, with equal time for each parent. Karen and her sister live six months with one parent and six months with the other parent. Holidays are equally divided, as is every second weekend. She thinks it's a great arrangement. Her parents live very close to each other.

At first a lot of people find that visiting is not regular. Some reported an initial break of up to six months before they saw their absent parent again. This may sound horrible, if you imagine not seeing one of your parents for six months to a year. However, I am told that this break can often be good as it allows some of the anger and hurt to subside. Jill didn't see her father for six months after he first left: "Of course, I wanted to see him after he left but that certainly wasn't the first thing I thought." The break seemed to give Jill and her mother time to get together: "It's unbelievable how well my mother and I get along. But the greatest thing is I get along with Dad much, much better now."

Jeff and Gord are both 18 and live on their own. Jeff's father lives in another city. Jeff goes to see his mother about once a week and travels to see his father one weekend a month. Gord can't see his mother very often as she lives too far away, so he makes sure he keeps in contact with his father regularly. Elizabeth's father is also out-of-town. She recommends that in these circumstances you should plan to go to visit for the whole weekend: "If it's a shorter time it's not worth the trip." Her father doesn't mind if she brings a friend along to keep her company on the bus.

Parents don't seem to mind your bringing friends for a visit, but they probably won't encourage you. Remember, just as it's hard on you to have your mother's boyfriend around every time you visit her, sometimes she would like to be alone with you without your friends.

What if your father seems more interested in visiting with his girlfriend than he does with you? Sharon's dad thought he was making her visit more pleasant when he would arrange that both Sharon and he go to his girlfriend's apartment. His girlfriend had a daughter Sharon's age: "He always dumped me with this kid and went to talk with his girlfriend. It was really boring. I finally told him, 'When I visit with you

I want to see you.' He changed a lot — we go places now, not just to her place." Generally this seems to be the rule: if you're having trouble with the visiting, tell your parent. If you'd rather just go over and do your homework, fine.

What most people seem to miss is the sense of being with their absent parents. Sometimes it's better, especially at first when visiting feels so weird and strange, not to do anything too special. Linda finds it best "just to be in the room next to my dad. If he's watching T.V. or something I know he's there. That's what I miss since he moved away. I just like having him around."

Everyone I spoke to agrees that arragements for visiting should be flexible. Usually your parent will phone to make arrangements or just to chat, or you can phone. It's important to be able to say "No" if you have other plans. But as Annette points out, "You should try to go once in a while to visit. If you don't want to go you shouldn't be forced, but it's not fair to the other parent if you don't go once in a while. When you're grown up you might want that extra person with you."

When making arrangements, talk directly with your absent parent. It can lead to all kinds of difficulties when your resident parent is involved. Jeff lives by himself, while his brother and sister live with his father in another city. When Jeff goes to visit his mother, in yet another city, he would like his brother and sister to come along too, so it could be more of a family thing. But when he calls his father there is difficulty in arranging this: "My father tries to prevent my brother and sister from visiting my mother. He's a bugger. He says they've got things to do, but they know if they want to come. I phone every week and ask." Jeff might try direct contact with his brother and sister who, being adolescent themselves, can make their own desires known to Jeff and to their father.

Special visits and holidays

Don't expect holidays to be the same. Before the separation the entire family used to get together for holidays like Christmas or Thanksgiving. For most people these were happy times and grandparents were often involved in the celebration. After the separation some families have attempted to retain the old rituals of getting together, while others try various alternate holidays like a trip to Florida or going skiing. While the holiday is still good, the family atmosphere of to-getherness seems to be missing. "Christmas didn't turn into a family thing, it didn't sparkle — it was just peculiar."

One thing no one misses are the fights that often come at times of stress, as on birthdays. Jill, an only child, misses the sense of family less than most: "When I was with my father, just the two of us, we got along fabulously. But when it was the three of us, it is un-believable how tense it was. Every special occasion was ruined. I dreaded birthdays and Christmases because there's that special kind of anticipation that this is going to work out wonderfully but it never did. There was always some kind of nit-picky thing that would happen. My father delegated me garbage girl, so whenever there were wrappings or any bits of anything that fell on the floor between gifts or between even words, he would yell at me to take them away. And he was just incredibly tidy. Sometimes we'd go over to the grandparents. I didn't like to 'cause my father hated them and they hated my father. Now, after the separation, it's very special with just Mother."

While Jill's experience is not unusual, by the time you are about 13 or 14 a family birthday celebration may not be as important. You may want to do your own planning with your own friends. Similarly with summer holidays, you have summer jobs by age 16 or even 14, so a more traditional family vacation is disrupted by this as much as by your parents' separation. Some of the group found that a good time to plan a more extended visit with an out-of-town parent is before summer employment starts.

How about concerts, sports events or graduations where you'd like both parents to see you? This is not always possible. Three of five people report that their parents refuse to attend the same event on the same night. If it goes for two nights they make appropriate arrangements. But if it's just a one-time thing you have to accept the fact that it's probably the parent you're living with who'll go. But even this can lead to communication difficulties. Richard plays hockey and is free to invite both parents. However, if his father is going his mother arranges to sit on the opposite side of the arena: "My mother would go but she'd ask if my father was going to be there. She'd always ask but if he didn't go she'd always ask, *'Why* didn't he go?' "

If only one parent goes you may find yourself becoming more distant from the other one. Elizabeth experienced this: "My parents will not see each other. If it's a two-day thing, like choir at school, it's okay. My father won't go unless my mother is not going. He doesn't go but I wish he would. Also, he's too busy and too far away. He can't be hassled with my social activities. We don't have time to sit down and keep up-to-date." It seems unfortunate that Elizabeth's father is missing out on some of the most important events and times of her life. It is then difficult for them to talk even about relatively superficial pleasant topics, much less to open channels for deeper communication and understanding. The group feels that, if possible, both parents should come. "They don't have to sit together."

Divorced families "celebrate" one other event. The anniversary of the separation is often marked by a comment from one or other parent: "Do you know what today is?" "Yeah, one of the worst days I've had all year." "Well, it's two years now, today is October 10th." Sharon says: "You are going to remember it for the rest of your life. I remember it's the last day of school, so I think about it at the end of the school year. I don't exactly celebrate, but I remember."

Feelings

The first visit with a parent outside the home almost always seems strange. I'm told it feels like going to a relative's, like an aunt's or uncle's, and sometimes people say it feels a bit lonely after one comes back from the visit. This passes quickly if both parents want you to visit and aren't jealous or afraid of your visiting.

Some parents seem to be afraid that if their child visits the other parent, they will be "won over" to that side and not love them anymore. Gord's father asks, "How was your time with your mother? Did she say anything about me?" The adolescents I spoke to rejected the idea that they can be influenced to such an extent. They feel that, given the correct information, most teenagers respond very rationally and with a great deal of insight and understanding for their parents' position. Richard found it took two years to get over the strange formal feelings when visiting his dad. His mother would make snide remarks when he was going to visit and sometimes afterwards when he'd talk about the visit. He found out that if he'd had a good time and shared this with his mother on his return, she became angry: "If I say something good about my dad she tells me all the bad things he's done. This can start an argument to this day." Richard now doesn't let his mother know if he's going to visit his dad. This leads to less friction. I heard from many of the young people that this is what they do. They described it as "cheating".

While this may be the only solution in some cases, in order to protect both your parents and your own feelings, I would like to suggest that before you resort to this you try talking to your parent. For example, Richard could tell his mother how he wants to be free to visit his dad and intends to continue to do so. He can let her know he appreciates her resentment and pain and that he cares for her even though he is continuing to see his dad. He can offer his mother a realistic choice. Would she prefer him not to mention his visits or if she wants him to honestly state where he's been would she agree not to berate his father? Parents tend to value honesty highly and are more distressed by their children lying to them than they are by their having a good relationship with the absent parent.

If you're 15 or younger you may find that your whereabouts are more carefully monitored and you do not have the option to visit when you choose. In this circumstance, if your parent gets tense when you talk about the terrific time you had on your visit, you might be advised to keep your descriptions to a minimum. If asked how the visit was you can reply simply, "Okay."

If your parent probes further or asks specific questions, they must bear the responsibility for any feelings of anger that they experience as a result of your honest reporting.

Some parents don't like to hear anything about their former partners. "They refuse to see each other and whenever I talk about my mum to my dad I can just feel him tense up. I feel like saying some snappy comment. I can just feel that happen. As a result I cannot share one of the important parts of my life, that is, my mother, with another important part of my life, my father, and vice versa. I just can't share it and that hurts. It really hurts."

You may find your parent wanting a lot of information about how the other parent is getting on. There may be other motives behind these questions. If a parent has left the home he or she may want to know that everything is going well. This seems to be motivated by guilt for leaving. Marion explains that it's "the person who leaves who doesn't mind hearing, the one who is rejected who doesn't want to hear. See, it helps their guilt feelings when the other person is going out. With my dad, one of the few times I talked to him since the divorce; I asked him why he was not helping out. He said he felt too guilty." This guilt reaction seems a pretty important factor in understanding why some parents react the way they do. For example, why they seem to avoid the family, don't call much, have difficulty with visiting. This parent might be devastated if you become angry or resentful of his or her behavior: "It doesn't hurt my mother if I like Dad's new girlfriend but it would hurt my father if my sister and I told him about my mother's new boyfriend."

On the other hand, the parent who is resentful or

hurt may have great difficulty in accepting your enjoying a visit with the other parent. When a parent is
experiencing hurt he or she may react by not wanting
the absent parent to know about the pain. For example,
Barbara's mother says, "Don't say anything to your
father. I don't want him knowing anything about me."
When Barbara returns home she feels like she's getting
the "third degree". She says: "That's two-faced. I hate
that kind of double message." Jill's mother wanted her
to tell her father what a great time they are having
without him. She wanted her to say, "I'm glad you left,
we're okay." Jill decided not to transmit this kind of
message because she feels this would make her part of a
triangle.

One of the situations that arouses a great deal of
feeling is meeting with the absent parent's girlfriend or
boyfriend, particularly if they are living in a common-
law union. Although this is gone into in more detail in
the chapter on dating and remarriage, a word about
handling visiting arrangements in this situation might
be appropriate here. You may find yourself experiencing a great deal of resentment and anger
towards your parent's new partner. Barry remembers
how he felt at first: "After they separated my father
went to live with his girlfriend and they're like that
right now — I see him once a week, maybe once every
two weeks. It's not designated or anything like that.
His girlfriend has a daughter by a previous husband
that died and I wouldn't want his girlfriend and her
daughter to go through what I did. I had terrible
feelings towards them at the beginning. I felt so
aggressive. You'd see people coming up to them and
saying, 'Hullo Mr. and Mrs. Cranbook,' and you want
to tell the person, 'Hey, this lady's got nothing to do
with this guy,' but after a while you realize that she's in

love with him and it's not her fault. If she wasn't there somebody else would have been and I guess I began to like them. I wouldn't want the same thing to happen to them."

Court ordered visiting

Most young people can't or won't be forced to do anything they don't want to do. So, when I asked the group about the courts' place in planning for visiting it was not surprising that I received comments like, "The court has no business being involved." "Custody's one thing — visiting should be entirely one's own opinion. Visiting rights are only assessed in court when the parents are ridiculous about their kids. That's not fair. I think these rules are made up for people who can't smarten up and act civilized. I know some adopted kids whose parents separated and their mother wants them to see their father. I think that's good. And the kids, they want to see everybody. I think there is no such thing as a visiting *right*. What right! I think it's important that a kid see his parent on his own when he wants to." Just as there is no "painless" divorce, there are no ideal visiting arrangements, whether established by the court or not.

The people I spoke with felt that to be forced to visit can make you resentful about going. Suppose you are ordered by the court to spend part of your summer holiday with your absent parent and you have a job or summer school. Let's say your absent parent lives in another city. What could you do? Slightly over half our group felt that you shouldn't go. Various alternate suggestions were made. You could go at another time or your parent could come to visit you. A really interesting idea was to extend your winter holiday by one or two weeks. If you're a good student you can usually get the extra time off, taking a week at the end of the holiday. Provided there aren't exams or something special this could be a very equitable solution. People who approached the school and talked frankly with the teachers or principal found them to be most helpful and understanding.

One of the times a court order for visiting may be valuable is when one parent is withholding visiting rights. This seems to be more of a problem for younger adolescents. Marion feels that "the agreement for visiting can force the parent to do something when they might not want to. If there is no problem with the parents' communication then it's not necessary."

Support payments

How about the mother who asks her kids not to visit because their father hasn't kept up his support payments? Jill says, "It's fair. If the parent isn't supporting why should they have the satisfaction of being with them? Maybe he should have thought of that when he left." Richard thinks, "Money shouldn't have anything to do with this. They are two different things. Both parents should be able to work it out unless one's a drunken bum or something like that." Here is one of the situations where you have to "check out your priorities." One group meeting we had got into a really heated argument on this point. According to Marion, "You must decide what's best for you. What's best for you might be what's good for the people around you. You have to measure things and think ration- ally — not about yourself first all the time. Remember people around you are going through the same thing.

You may need money — that's one thing — but you have an obligation to see your parents."

Elizabeth: "I know someone whose mum got them to go to the dad and tell him how poor they were. I wouldn't do that. I'll fight for what I believe in. The mother should deal with it directly."

Marion: "Not if you didn't want to do it. But if you were really poor and it is only for you, it's okay to drop a hint. I'd tell Mum to go to a lawyer or to a mutual friend who could let him know how bad things are."

Richard: "I wouldn't do it. I want to be uninvolved. Both my parents are broke. My mum has been hounding me to find out if my dad's got a job. I just shrug it off. It doesn't go past the walls of the house."

Margaret: "That's just the same thing as my father. He's absolved himself from every financial thing as regards the house and us kids. My mother says, 'I don't believe you should be going down there,' but I don't think she should have any say."

Bob: "It's not as if a father is paying to see his child. Why should he have to pay? It's just silly, your friends don't have to pay to see you. Why should your dad have to pay?"

So it seems that the general conclusion is that visiting should be a child's or adolescent's right — not so much a parental right. As a general rule, if visiting rights are being contested in the courts, it's a case where the parents' rancor is interfering in their understanding of their children's desires. If this happens you might try and understand your parents are hurt and angry and using the question of visiting rights to strike out at each other. Of course, you're not a possession like a car or a boat or a house. If you get yourself heavily involved in the financial aspects of a separation you may well find yourself being treated like a stick of furniture. This is not to say you don't have a place in the family financial matters: you do. You will probably be much more aware of the family's financial state than your friends are. You may well contribute income to the family or pay your own expenses to help out. But stay clear of the legalities if you can.

ADVICE ON VISITING:

For adolescents
1   Don't lose contact. Keep your visiting fairly regular or you'll find yourself drifting away from your absent parent.
2   Keep the visiting arrangements — and the visits themselves — simple at first.
3   Call your absent parent and tell them if you want to see them. Remember that he or she may be busy and say "No", but you'll be unavailable sometimes too.
4   Don't deliver verbal messages, letters or cheques.
5   If your parent remarries, keep the first few visits short. Give them a chance to get together. They will be more able and ready to include you in a month or two. (This may not apply if you've known the new partners for some time.)

For parents

1 Try to spend some time alone with your son or daughter occasionally, even if the conversation lags and you don't know what to say.

2 Teenagers understand business and other commitments and that you are not always available. What they like is clear planning from their parents. Don't be disappointed if they can't arrange to meet you on short notice, or if they don't give you the same courtesy but cancel at the last minute. It's not that they don't care but that they often lead pretty active lives.

3 Keep up with their social events and achievements. Try to attend important events even if your former spouse will be present.

8
Your Parents Before and After.

"Before and after" sounds like an ad for a fitness center. While it may be true for many parents that a separation or divorce is just the first step to a healthier, happier future, as you know, not all parents are left with a positive outlook. What changes can you expect in your relationship with your parents and how can you help them to adjust to their new way of life? Judging from what the adolescents in the group said, the change, if any, in your relationship with each parent will depend on your sex, your parent's sex and whether or not you are living in the same household.

Mothers

The girls who are living with their mothers generally report that their mothers are more trusting, more open and closer to them than before the separation. Elizabeth's relationship with her mother is a good example: "I think we're a lot closer than when we were together as a family. Now we talk about more personal experiences and, if we need it, hug each other. We just ask for it — we've become mother-daughter but also close friends because there's no other adult in the home to talk to. My sister doesn't get the same because she doesn't have the wide view." Marion says: "My mother and I have benefited. We have had to realize a lot about ourselves. My mother and I are more of a team. It's really fun to get to know her that way."

Despite this new closeness, some of the girls, like Abby, found their mothers were still able to retain a parenting role: "My mother is really the parent in the family, telling us to practice the piano and pick up our things. She's got to do all the raising and bringing us up. We can be friends sometimes and then after she realizes what's happening and she'll assume her authority over me and she'll get mad at me. I want to give her more than she has because she deserves more."

Boys who are living with their mothers have gained a great respect for them after seeing them take on the challenges of running a house alone and bringing up the children as well. Richard says: "I've always had respect for my mother. Our relationship is still a mother-son relationship. A lot of times I advise her but at times she'll say, 'You're not bringing me up — I'm bringing you up.' She wants a bigger mother-son gap. Sometimes all of us try to make it so we can talk to her but she resists that." John finds that his mother has more respect for his opinion as well: "It's a lot more one-to-one, a lot more equal. I have a lot to say."

Joel felt that living with his mother and wanting to maintain a good relationship with her prevented him from visiting his father as much as he would have wished. Michael had the same feeling: "I am closer with my mother, happier. I always got along with her — I really don't go to see my father because it would upset her. I should have gone. I know that now."

Karen is the only girl in the group living with her father. She feels that her mother pays too much attention to her younger sister, babies her in a way. But other than that she see no change. Boys living with their fathers, as Jerry, Jim and Harold are, seem to have lost some of the mother-son relationship: they see their mothers more as adults. Jim says: "I'm more like a good friend. She doesn't treat me like a son anymore. She does when it's good to. I enjoy being treated like a son. But when we go places it's just like good friends."

Fathers

On the whole, the group of adolescents I spoke with were much less positive about their relationships with their fathers.

Among the boys living with their fathers, Harold is angry about his father's girlfriend and her two daughters. Of his father he says: "He's a ladies' man and I'm just an object in the house." But Jim and Jerry speak in much the same terms as the girls who are living with their mothers. "I listen to what he says and he treats me like a son. I think that's right," says Jim, while Jerry feels that his father has become more of a friend.

Even if they didn't do so at first, the boys who visit their fathers regularly have become closer and more understanding. Richard explains how this happened for him: "I didn't see him in the first year. At the end of the year I needed a new suit for graduation so I phoned my dad and asked if he could buy me one and that was the first time I saw him. It was strange. It was more like a friend rather than a father. Before, he

had always been at work. It didn't bother me, his leaving. I never felt I missed him. But lately I do. I've noticed my friends' families. I'm seeing him a lot more and he's helping me a bit. We are not so far apart."
Even though Bob is seeing his father less often, he feels there is more mutual understanding: "My relationship with my father has strengthened tremendously. It's a much better relationship now than it was before, although I don't see him as often as I used to before, you know, coming home for dinner and things like that. I see him right now usually once a week. He has moved farther away. Our relationship is now more an adult-to-adult friendship. We are closer."

If your father and you don't keep in touch early on, it seems hard to get back together later. Richard was fortunate, but Michael talks about how much he feels he has missed over the years: "In my case, I never felt that close to my father and it was hard imagining a relationship with him after we were separated. I didn't see him right away but I did speak to him a couple of times. I suppose my father felt threatened and I feel sorry for him now. I wonder why I didn't continue any relationship with him afterwards but we didn't have all that much in common. I suppose he was hoping for me to come around. I had to come around on my own. But I didn't because I was happier the way things were, I suppose. It was quiet and there were no hassles. He called me up recently and asked me how I'd been and stuff and asked me if I wanted to go and see him. We haven't seen each other yet but I know already what it will be like. We'll go out and we'll sit and talk about school and things like that. He'll say, 'Why don't we have a normal son-father relationship?' and I'll say, 'I don't know,' and he'll say, 'I'd like to see you more,' and I'll say, 'I suppose so,' but I won't really get around to calling him. I'm selfish maybe but I don't want to get involved in his problems. I don't feel any need for him. There was a time when I was younger that I really felt the need for a father, that is, I felt a need to communicate with both parents. I also wanted a close relationship with my father, being able to talk to him. I felt a need for a father — not necessarily him.''

Laurie's relationship with her father is much the same, although Laurie seems to be holding on to her anger more. Even though she realizes what is happening it seems hard to break the pattern: "He wanted us to go over to his house. I hated this man who had completely destroyed my life, or so I thought. On my birthday, he came into the store where I was working. He spoke with the manager and said it was my birthday and he had something for me. He put on a real sad sack act. He gave me this gift and I unwrapped it. It was a stuffed animal. Well, I collect them and I've got about 50. This was one I didn't have and I was really torn. I gave it back to him and said I didn't want it — I didn't want anything from him. He'd never really been good to me in the past months, so why should he start now? He put on a few tears which I did not believe, but I gave in. I took the animal and I threw it in with the rest of them. My mother was quite upset over the whole thing. She was saying that I must be changing my way of life if I was accepting things from my father. I see my father now and we still argue. My father can't understand why I'm not willing to forget the past. A lot of my friends think I'm wrong, but it's hard to put the past out. He keeps calling. I went out to dinner with him once and he wanted to meet my boyfriend and all. I suppose it's wrong. I should let the past be the past. Sometimes I feel sorry for him. When he calls I feel guilty and go to see him and I think I'm stupid to go because of guilt, not because I want to."

Many of the girls found it awkward and even scary to go and visit with their fathers. Elizabeth explains how the anxiety has grown until she now feels she doesn't love her father: "Before separation he was father on weekends. We'd do things together. Now I don't look on him as a father — he's a father in name. I don't love him as much as Mom because there's not as much contact. He doesn't know what I think. In a sense I'm scared and nervous of him. He does his duties as a father but I don't consider him a father. We just can't seem to get together. I haven't really loved him in seven years."

Margaret and Abby also have this sense of shyness around their fathers. One cause seems to be the awkwardness that comes with talking to an adult who knows very little about you. You can help your father by filling the gaps even if you think he might find it boring to hear all about school, your friends and activities. Margaret says, "About a year after they separated I started to go and see my father. He's so shy around me he doesn't know what to talk to me about, you know. He can't talk to me about school because he feels that ties in with the separation and he doesn't want to talk about that. It's just made me feel so uncomfortable and I feel that if, you know, I feel that he's been embarrassed by my mother for being kicked out of his house. Then to be embarrassed in front of his children and in front of, you know — and that's really bad because I know what my father thought of me when I was smaller. He always used to get me out of trouble with my mother. Sometimes I look at him as if I've never seen him before in my life. I really feel it's bad that I knew everything about the marriage breakup. It's really bad for students. I think it's better just to know the general reason.''

As well as telling your father about all your interests you will want to get to know him too if you are to feel really comfortable with one another. Abby has some trouble assimilating all the changes in her father: "I remember when I started to see my dad on Saturdays it was really, really strange because here was a man that I had never really known before. I knew one of the whole reasons for my parents separating is because he was never at home. He was setting up his new business and I was almost scared of him because I was alone. I wasn't with my mom and here was this person I had to face. My sister was just two at the time and, you know, she couldn't really do much, so it was just he and I and sometimes I was scared and it took such a long adjustment period to get used to him, to get used to seeing him, and it was quite difficult at first. He always felt he had to take us places, be like an ideal father, because he had never really been a father before. He was entertaining us but he would always say how much he loved me and it was really awkward because I didn't know what to say back. I really didn't. I didn't know him and still now we know each other a lot better, but when he says 'I love you' I still feel awkward because I still don't feel that I know him enough. My dad is really changing. He's started to go to the synagogue and he's started to become religious."

Although some of the girls had concerns about visiting their fathers, some found that they got along much better after the separation. Jill is one of these girls: "The greatest thing is, I get along with my father much better now. Because I don't have him eagle-eyeing everything I do all the time. Although he was very liberally minded, having him gone, discussions are so much more special and I don't get any flak. This is not my imagination. My friends who'd come over were embarrassed by the way he picked on me. Now it's changed and I can even take my friends over to his place. Before he left I could never truly say I loved my father. Now I really can. That's a good feeling but it's too bad that I can't tell that to my mother — that I love him — because she would be hurt. He still criticizes me sometimes, sure, but I don't worry. I feel more secure. It's more like a friend than a parent.''

Worries

It's normal for adolescents to begin to realize that their parents aren't perfect. As a child you may have felt that your parent could solve any problem you might bring to him or her, whether it was a cut finger or a math problem. Gradually, you realize they don't have all the answers. If your parents get a divorce you may find yourself catapulted into the realization that your parents could be in very serious difficulty for which they don't have solutions. You might tend to become very worried about a parent who is having financial or emotional problems.

Approximately half the group worried about their mothers' financial position, while only two people were concerned for their fathers'. This view has made some people quite resentful of their father's position. Barry says: "He has a well-paying job. He doesn't want to pay her alimony. They are always arguing back and forth through the lawyers. I think she's getting the bum steer." While Abby feels her mother has other options, she is angry at her father for not helping out: "To an extent I'm worried about her (my mother).

She's had lots of chances to do something about her situation. She could sell the house and buy a smaller one and have it paid for. But she's kind of clinging to it. She could get out of debt. My father has more money than he knows what to do with. He quit paying support."

Although Gord doesn't know how much actual financial difficulty his mother is in, he worries: "She's lived in a small town out West now for six years. I wonder how she survives. She just had an operation and missed a lot of work. I think she lost her job."

Annette and Elizabeth worry about how hard their mothers work. Elizabeth states: "I worry she's working too hard. Her social life — I wish she didn't have such financial pressures on her. She's got two jobs. I took one over because of income tax. I wish I could help her but I can't. I wish I could reach out and take all her troubles away but I can't. I pray for her every night. She's a workaholic. I wish she could stop."

A lot of people I spoke with worried about their parents being left alone when all the children leave home. People were also worried that parents living alone might become depressed. Jerry says: "Yeah, the loneliness. He doesn't go out and he doesn't date. I figure five years from now there's not going to be anybody at home and what's he going to do? That worries me." Michael: "I wonder what will happen to my mother when she's alone. My two sisters have moved out and I will be going off to university next year. In about three years I'll be out on my own. How will she get along by herself? She needs us not only for help around the house but she'll feel alone. It's easier when parents are together and have someone. I suppose it happens in any family. You feel you are justified in wanting your freedom, a life of your own, but you worry. I have thought about talking to my sisters lately about our sharing this responsibility for Mom, but one sister is going to live in Israel and the other is married."

The adolescents in the group were very concerned if their parents were depressed, particularly if the parents were using drugs and alcohol to combat depression. Jeff recalls: "He threatened my mother with a gun. I worry he'll put a gun to his own head if even two of his children leave. He went into a large depression one time. I still worry about him." Barbara says: "I worry about him drinking himself into the slums. I'm always worried he could be driving a car. Even if he was drunk at least you felt safe when he was home. I always knew when he was home because my mother would climb into bed with me. He could be sitting in his apartment dead for a month and I wouldn't know." Although Jim's worries for his father are not life-and-death issues, he still finds himself thinking about his dad: "I worry about my father. My dad sometimes seems depressed and I wonder whether he is going to have trouble. He gets depressed when he works a lot and loses sleep and what's going to happen to him after the second divorce and things like that. But he'll make it. I just worry a change with him will affect me too."

Help for your parents

Should you expect yourself to be able to advise or help your parent with his or her worries? Probably not. Your parents may not want to burden you with all their worries, so you will be handicapped in offering a useful opinion. If you are asked for your opinion you may wish to handle the situation as Elizabeth does: "I give my opinion. I give them both guidance but I do not tell them what to do."

Getting too involved can sometimes cause problems. Harold says: "My mother calls me two-faced because she thinks I do things for my father I wouldn't do for her. What can I say? She's not me. But I can't make her believe that I care for her. I guess I'm not good at speaking about my problems. My mother got all worried how we felt, my sister and my brother and I. She always gets hurt. That's her problem. I can't seem to help her. She doesn't worry about herself enough." Marion found that while she can help her mother by listening, at times she gets overburdened: "My mother tells me her feelings and I've appreciated that. It helps me to understand so I can live my life and I can help her to help herself. At times, I felt like the force to keep the whole family together. At one time I told them to stop putting pressure on me — then I said, 'O.K. now I'm ready!' "

Of course it's important to understand what your parents are going through and to help in any way you can. But acting as your parent's counsellor may not be in anybody's best interest. What are some of the other ways your parents might get help? Four out of five adolescents in the group said that one or both of their parents had sought professional help through a psychiatrist, a psychologist, a minister or a marriage counsellor. I asked if anyone saw an affect on their parents as a result of counselling. Sixty-one percent felt that counselling had had no effect. Some people were not sure if it helped and others clearly felt it had helped their parents deal with their own feelings. Would they advise other people to urge their parents to seek professional counselling? Five out of eight people said they wouldn't recommend marriage counselling because it didn't work, but some felt it might help parents sort out their feelings afterwards.

Dawn felt her mother got a lot of help by joining a group for single parents: "After about a year and a half my mom joined the One Parent group. They have adult activities and family activities. There's just a bunch of people and they have a good time. They have a lot of dances. My mom has really benefited from this group, knowing that there's a lot of other people like her that want to try to adjust and make the best out of it. And my mom thinks that this group is really good. Nobody talks about how they're divorced and separated or anything. Everybody just goes and has a good time." You might want to encourage your parents to get into outside activities. Just as it can help you to have new interests, so it can be good for your mother or father.

Friends can be most helpful to your parents as sounding boards. Maybe they can talk more freely about their feelings to an adult friend than they can to you. Margaret says: "My mother's friends were really supportive to her and me." And Barbara notes: "My mother talks to her friends when she's angry. She says the anger builds up and that's her way of getting it out." Tragically, family friends often take sides. This can be very painful for everyone. Annette recalls: "Some of my parents' friends took sides. Like, some good friends of my mom's don't talk to my dad and some good friends of my dad's don't talk to my mom. I think it's pretty hard on my parents because we don't see these friends and neither do my parents."

You may want to encourage your mother or father to turn to their relatives for support — if these relatives understand your parent's need for support. Sometimes relatives can behave very strangely in a family crisis, as Jim describes: "My mom's sister disowned her. They used to be really close. But now they don't talk to each other. I don't know whether she's on my dad's side or whether it was because of the kids. She's never experienced a divorce, so how does she know?" Harold found his grandmother equally lacking in understanding: "My grandmother is very religious so after the divorce she never invited us to dinner any more. She'd always ask us: 'Why can't we all get back together and live in the same house?' "

The unpredictable ways in which relatives react to a crisis can sometimes be helpful. Barry says: "A funny thing happened with my father's mother — she became much better friends with my mother. I guess because there wasn't the competition between her and my mother and now they are good friends. But, of course, now she's become enemies with my father's girlfriend." I guess it would be too much to hope that all relatives and friends could react with help and care the way Jerry's aunt did: "I have an aunt, a close friend really, but I call her 'Aunt'. She stepped in and talked to both my father and mother. She's known my father all her life. She spoke to them both often and still does. She doesn't have much effect on my mother."

Bitterness

One of the most difficult tasks is attempting to deal with the bitterness of one or both parents that is all too often the aftermath of a divorce. Parents generally start out trying to be fair and to help their children see both sides, but with courts, support payments and lawyers, bitterness often emerges. Jerry remembers: "At first my dad didn't seem bitter, but after the heat started he'd get mad and yell and scream. He wouldn't want to say bad things about her in front of us. If he ever did he would correct himself. If I was going through a time when I wouldn't speak to my mom he would always say, 'She's still your mother and try and speak to her.' "

Bob says: "My mother is more subtle. She knows I wouldn't take her saying things about my dad. If she did I'd get mad. It's strictly between my mother and father. There would be a scene. I'd ask her what she means." One of the difficulties with the bitterness is its infectious nature. John describes how his father's bitterness began to reflect in his mother's behavior: "My father was so bitter he tried to influence me. I'd be really up during the week and then I'd go to my father's on the weekend and get really down. Like, at one point, it was getting so bad my mother was going to stop me seeing him. At first, Mother tried not to say anything about him no matter what. Lately, he's been so awful she's fed up."

Nancy says this is one problem adolescents can't help their parents with. She says you just have to protect yourself. Margaret agrees: "The more you offer to help, the more they ask. Everything that goes wrong is his fault. If the car doesn't start, 'That bum left me with a bum car.' He didn't leave her with anything. You just have to listen and let it blow away." Sharon admits that sometimes she feels hurt: "Well, sometimes I go to my room and cry. I let her know how much it hurts for her to do that." Jim says, "Parents know they shouldn't do these things but they still do. It's pretty confusing. It's not black and white. You have to find out for yourself and make your own decision." Richard understands why his mother "calls my dad every name in the book. She's just hurt because he left. I try to understand."

One of the great problems with this kind of bitterness is that it doesn't always subside. Although Michael's mother now appears to be encouraging him to visit his father, her anger is just beneath the surface: "She had so much trouble getting him to support us. Maybe she felt bad when we expressed interest in going to see him. That bothered me because I felt that she shouldn't turn me against him or stop me from seeing him or make me feel bad when I wanted to see him, and she did that a lot. Now she says he's old and if I want to see him I should, because I might regret not knowing him. But she's still really bitter. If I say anything positive about him she says, 'If you like him so much why don't you go and live with your father?' "

I can only suggest that if you find that one parent is expressing a great deal of bitterness you encourage that parent to take their problem outside the family to a relative, a responsible family friend or a counsellor. You can let your parent know how upsetting and disturbing it is for you to see them in so much pain and anguish and to hear them saying things about your other parent. Marion describes this pain well: "Bitterness doesn't go away. It's like death — it's a pain you have to live with. In some ways it's worse than death 'cause it's living still. You see the person. Then all the hurt comes back. It's just awful. You lose the person and you're left with all the hurt. You're reminded all the time. At first, it's the child's responsibility not to talk too much about the absent parent. Let the parent get used to the idea of who you are living with — it helps a parent to be less rivalrous — maybe not visit for a while — makes Mom more secure. My mom fears everytime my sister visits my father she's going to stay forever."

ADVICE ON HELPING PARENTS:

For adolescents

1 Try to understand. Don't judge your parents too harshly: they're only people.
2 When visiting your parent don't be afraid of boring him or her. Keep talking about yourself.
3 Encourage your parents to get involved in outside activities.
4 Listen, and encourage your parents to use other sympathetic ears as well.

For parents

1 You may be angry — and justifiably so — with your ex-partner. But don't punish your children by sharing your bitterness with them.

9

The Second Time Around.

When young children learn about the facts of life they often find they can believe the information but can't imagine that their own parents have sexual relations. It's okay for the birds and the bees, but not for Mummy and Daddy. Some are even quite shocked. You may find yourself having the same kind of reaction when your parents start dating again. Although Jeff knew it was natural for his parents to want to date he says, "It was a shock at first for my mother to date but it doesn't bother me now. My dad dates but he's like a little kid about it. He never wants to tell me. He gets embarrassed. I like to see him date."

Like Jeff, most people are pleased when their parents start to date, even if it does seem a bit strange at first. Perhaps you may find yourself with some concerns about their dating: "I worry if one of my parents is going to be alone without other people but I had a lot of resentment when they started going out. I talked to other people and found out this was natural. Every time my mother meets someone I think it's going to be my step-father and I just jump to conclusions. I keep it in too much. I think I should talk it out more."

There seems to be a kind of ambivalent feeling of not wanting your parents to be alone and lonely, but resenting the implied replacement of your other parent. Abby found this: "When my parents started going out with other people, I felt confused and resentful. I didn't want this person entering. It has taken me a really long time to get used to my mom going out with other people. With my dad, he saw a few women. I thought they were trying to take the place of my mother and I was resentful because of that and I thought that I was betraying my mother if I liked them."

Dawn says, "Then my mom went out with some men, some other men. It sort of made us feel pretty bad but it made my mom a lot happier. She's always had to have a man. So, I think that when she was going out with some other men she probably felt pretty bad about it too. But you know, she wanted a man and like, she went out with a lot of other men. First she didn't for about a year. Then she started to adjust and everything when she sort of got used to the fact. Then she went out with a couple of different men. Then she had a permanent boyfriend, if you want to call it that, and they went a lot of places together. He had many children and there were some that were our age. We used to do things together and they got really close — my mom and this man. We, my sister and I, sort of worried that they'd get married and take the place of my father but we just didn't like the idea of another father. So they broke up and then got back together. Every time they broke up I'd say to myself, 'Oh, this is it! They'll never see each other again.' Finally that happened."

Everyone I spoke with had completely accepted their parents' separation. No one was involved in trying to get their parents back together. A very few did try for the first little while but certainly by one year following the separation they were more concerned about their parents being alone. Barry worries: "My mom's not dating. I worry that after I leave (he's the youngest with two older sisters), if she lives alone by herself, I'm not sure if that will be very good. My dad's fine but if he starts screwing around with somebody else it will mess up his life a lot. He's just moved in with his girlfriend." Jerry wants his father to date: "I think my dad should. He's only dated four times. He doesn't want to but I think he should. I'm concerned about his sex life."

Some of the older boys found themselves becoming quite protective of their mothers. Ted found that he was more aware of other men's interest in his mother than perhaps she was: "After a while I'd get used to a new person. If a guy is trying to move in on my mother I'm truthful with her. I just let her have the facts." The girls in the group seemed less concerned about their mothers, as did Elizabeth: "I know my mother can handle it. It's her responsibility if she wants to go out and have a close relationship with a man. I don't get frightened. She's old enough to know and that's fine."

Jill finds it difficult to accept when her mother dates socially without any seeming affection for her date: "I had to realize that Mom's a different person now. She's going to feel strange on a date. I love the idea of my parents dating but sometimes it turns sour. I don't like my mother's attitude about going out with guys. She teases guys. She is using him like he's a tool. I can't believe she does that. Those attitudes I can't stand in a woman. I don't appreciate that. But if she'd hidden her dating life, I wouldn't have such an all-round opinion. I don't respect at all what she's doing dating-wise. It sets the pattern for me. She'll always be okay, but not as happy or satisfied as she could be.''

It can seem strange when you find that your parents are enjoying dating, maybe even flirting. Not many people think of their parents in this way. For this reason, it might be wise not to be too much in evidence when your parents are just getting to know somone. As for going out on a double date with your parents, nine out of ten people agreed this could be a very awkward situation. Marion says, "I've seen some cases where the mother does stuff you shouldn't do in front of a son. It's really upsetting for the son. In the majority of cases it's not a good idea to get two generations mixed up. You need more separateness.'' Margaret feels the same way: "Suppose a guy goes out on a double date and his mother's a flirt. A guy's still young at 17. That's a general loss of respect for the kid on the part of the mother. He's still gathering ideas about women. His mother is the most important woman in his life.'' John took his girlfriend out on a date with his mother and her boyfriend: "It was not too good. My date was uptight. I never saw her again.'' Some people, like Barbara, feel awkward going out with their parents by themselves, so a dating situation would add even more strain: "I still feel really weird going out with my parents at all, much less on a date. It's okay if it's a celebration like a birthday or away like skiing.''

Suggestions for avoiding such invitations as "Bill and I are going to a movie Saturday. Why don't you invite Mary to come along?'' vary from saying you're sick, to saying you have other plans, to saying you don't want to go. Those people who favor making an excuse feel that total honesty might offend their parent. Others feel it might be best to clarify that you don't think it would be a good idea until you get to know your own date better as well as their date. Some people found that if their mother or father had been going out with someone for some time and they all got along well in more everyday situations, then it was okay to bring a date along. Richard states, "I went out with my dad and his new wife and my girlfriend. It was pretty casual and pretty easy. There was no problem — it was pretty relaxed. So dating can work sometimes."

When a parent starts dating, particularly if it's the parent you're not living with, you may find they have less time to spend with you. This can sometimes bring out feelings of jealousy, not toward the person but jealousy because of the time your parent spends with that person. "It was okay," Laurie says, "except when he met the girl. I don't know, it felt like he was a mess and not caring anymore. He just went over to the girl's place. We began to be friends with the girl. She's really nice, eh? And he started to see her more often and sometimes he forgot when we had our nights. Eventually he moved in with her. Lots of times we thought he didn't care because he was with her and that he was rejecting us." Even though a parent may be dating and have less time to spend with his or her children, this does not imply rejection. The attachment to one's own children is unique. Elizabeth understands this difference: "I've known from the beginning I've always had a special place. If I was ever in trouble my dad would be there."

But feelings of jealousy or competition for your parents' time can sometimes be heightened when the parent is dating a much younger person. The people in the group had very mixed feelings about parents having young dates. A man who is 38 may well have

teenage children of 16 or 17 and yet find himself attracted to a 22-year-old woman. Annette suspects the
motives of her dad's younger dates: "I don't tell my
dad's dates anything about him when they ask. I'm
suspicious of a young woman with my father. She
might be a gold-digger just trying to get a few things
out of it." When Abby's mother went out with a man
who was 24, Abby found, "He was able to get along
with both of us. Afterwards it didn't work out because
my mom had been through more than he had. She had
more experience. I knew he wasn't like my dad."

Harold feels very competitive with his dad's
girlfriend: "There's an age difference between my
father and his girlfriend of 13 years. I hate her. I try not
to get involved. I always have to compete for my
father's attention with his girlfriend. I think there's
more competition because she's closer in age to me."
Although Jill hasn't personally had this happen she
reacts rather strongly with an idea as to how we might
understand this: "I'd lose respect for my father if he
was being immoral in my eyes. It would definitely make
me lose respect. I'd be happier with my dad being gay
or going out with a series of mature women in a row
than going out with an 18-year-old. If a father does that
he obviously hasn't grown up. I have a friend whose
father flirts with all her girlfriends. It seems an attempt
to recapture youth. I guess it's like you're over the hill
and want to be a teenager again." Richard feels much
the same way: "I have a friend and her sister is going
out with a teacher. I can't see it. I can't imagine my
father doing that. It doesn't seem right. If Dad was
going out with someone at my school I'd say something
to him."

I asked what people thought they might do if faced
with this situation. Marion felt, "If I bring it up it

might alienate him. I can't help him. He's got to realize it on his own." Several people thought that this kind of situation was just not their business and felt they shouldn't get involved. "My mother's not living at home but we're really close. I'm glad she's dating even younger men. If she wants me to like him and if she likes him that's fine by me. It's her business." Jerry says, "I let Dad do what he wants. He has his life and I won't always be living with him. It doesn't bug me if she's in her 20's. It's none of my business. Just like he can't say who I can date. He's going to do what he wants."

The consensus of opinion is that parents should be free to choose whomever they wish to date. If you find the relationship particularly distressing, you might tell your parent about your feelings. One thing is clear. Parents have to do what they think is best for themselves at the time. You may just have to wait and see what happens. Expressing your opinions too strongly could hurt or embarrass your parent who, in turn, might react with anger at you. You know how you might feel if someone criticized your date.

No matter what age they are, your parents' dates may want to get to know you. Some people find that their parents' friends try to become buddies with them. Sometimes they seem to be using you, ingratiating themselves with you to get to your parent. Marion says, "There's really nothing wrong if a person tries to befriend another person on a casual basis. There's a certain amount that's acceptable, but I naturally suspect my dad's friends. I suspect a present — I feel like I'm being bought off."

I wondered if it might not be difficult to tell who was being truly friendly and who was using you. But

Barbara explains that teenagers have no difficulty recognizing phoniness: "If a front is being put up I recognize it. At first I have doubts and resent it. If they are fine with each other then I'd accept it. But if she was lying to get to me I would avoid her. It puts my father in a difficult position if I say anything to him. If it was a real thing between them it's not up to me to break it up. I'm not going to be around forever." Annette thinks much the same: "I try to trust Dad's judgment and just keep out of it."

But Jill says that when one of her mom's boyfriends was too friendly too fast, she talked it over with him: "I did that. It was over in ten minutes. I couldn't stand it when he was chummy — it was false. He was trying to relate to me on my level, trying to pretend that he's just like me. That turns me off right away. Because of his age he has a right to be different. It's so obvious if a person is pushing. Right away I know, when a new guy of my mother's walks in. I sense it right away from the first five sentences. 'When I was your age...' — cool it. When we first meet it's better to wait for me to start a conversation." Bev found herself afraid to get close to her mother's date because they might break up: "For a period of about two years my mom had been seeing a bunch of men and it made her happy and everything because she was really depressed about my father. First of all, she saw a man for about a year. Then he got back together with his wife. Then she started seeing this other man and then he got back together with his wife. Then she started seeing this other man. I was afraid for her that they'd break up or something. So I don't really get attached to the men that she goes out with."

Sex

Adolescents today are quite knowledgeable about sexual development. The people I spoke with had done a lot of thinking about sexual behavior and standards. They had developed their own individual ideas about what was correct social and sexual behavior and what was proper for their parents. Marion, though not sexually naive, found herself dumbfounded by her father's frank admission of his extra-marital affair: "When they were separating I asked my dad, 'Have you had an affair?' and he said 'Yes', and I was really shocked. I could hardly believe that he would stoop to such levels because at that point it started to seem like a bit of a soap opera and I was — I was disgusted and I should say shock and disgust were my first initial reactions. Those didn't last long. I started to think very quickly and to me it wouldn't have been nearly as serious — I guess I was naive in thinking this but if this affair just hadn't gone as far as sexual relations, yet it wouldn't be that bad and my dad would just move out to an apartment and everything would blow over. But I asked my dad, like, he said, and I said, 'Well I do have one thing to ask. Just don't sleep with your mistress until you're married or something.' He said, 'Well, I'm sorry but I already have,' and I was shocked — not shocked — but I was disappointed again. It just overwhelmed me and I was trying to uphold this pillar of strength image but it shattered, needless to say, and I just went outside crying. I think he had a lot of problems and he's sort of going through his adolescence or something like this, and I think he had a lot of problems growing old. This is a sort of starlet case. He had a lot of problems growing old and it was my theory that he probably wanted this boost of being young again and attractive to women. The thing is my dad has strict principles in his own way. So he couldn't have an affair and then go back to the old way of living."

While most people were pleased their parents were dating and understood their parents' sexual needs, they found themselves reacting rather strongly when their mother or father brought someone home to spend the night.

The following dialogue took place at one group meeting:

John: "Sex can be a shock. A guy would be on the couch — a real shocker. My mom talked about it later. Parents should keep kids aware."

Abby: "Parents should talk about it before sex. It's better. It makes it more normal. Parents have to realize it's a big adjustment. They have to talk about the way they feel."

Margaret: "As far as I'm concerned, she's told me too much already. I don't want to know details."

Nancy: "I live with my father and his girlfriend stays over. It's okay because I know they're going to get married."

Sharon: "If they're going to get married and you've got to cope with that every morning it's alright."

Margaret: "I don't like it at all. I feel sort of *super out of place.* I'm too conservative. I don't believe in premarital sex. I would feel like I was living in a commune. People come and people go. Suppose she brings home another guy. She should get the guy out before the kids get up."

It might help in the adjustment to remember that

what we are talking about is not premarital sex but postmarital sex. So standards you may have for yourself as a single person may not apply equally to a single but divorced parent.

In some cases the parents' failure to discuss the sexual aspect of their relationship led to some difficulties. Laurie and Joel have lost some respect for their parents, Laurie because her mother tries to shield her, and Joel because his parents haven't dealt with it directly: "I began to do things subconsciously to strike back. I began to steal money from my mother because I couldn't trust her anymore because I caught her in the living-room with a man. The man also happens to be a friend of mine. At that point I played dumb and pretended that I didn't know what was going on, so as not to cause any confusion. To me there was no positive proof that my father had done these things but when I had actually caught my mother in the act it upset me. My sister — she's 18 — had told me my father was an adulterer. It kind of hit me like a solid brick wall. I began not to trust my father. I began to learn things about my father and I'd realize that there were a lot of women in his life. I realized in a sense my dad couldn't help himself." Laurie realizes that having normal sexual responses, following a marital relationship of some years, means that her mother is probably having sex with her boyfriend: "She always says she hasn't let Karl touch her. She thinks it's wrong. But I don't believe that. She can't be stupid. He's had five kids. She just had a miscarriage. She's not stupid like she lets on. I believe she's had sexual relationships with Karl. She won't admit it. It doesn't bother me if she would have sex — it's not going to break my image. The only thing is that she thinks she's doing wrong and when things go bad between her and Karl, it will crush her."

Judging from these reactions, it would seem that you will be most comfortable with your parents' sexual life if you understand that a sexual relationship is a normal part of an adult postmarital attachment. You might prefer that they not bring their boyfriend or girlfriend home unless they are planning a more permanent arrangement. But this may not suit you either. Richard says, "Sometimes she stays out all night — just doesn't come home. I worry about whether she'll be all right. I think about it. I worry because she has no steady boyfriend and yet she stays out all night."

It seems each person has to reconcile their own moral precepts and, if these differ markedly with their parents, talk it over with them. If you decide to speak to your parent about his or her sexual life they may find this intrusive and be less than frank. Alternatively, as with Margaret's mother, you may get too many details for your liking. I'd suggest that you put boundaries on your discussion before you begin. You might want to say, "Mom, I want to talk to you about George and you. You've been going out with him some time now and I imagine some weekends when I'm away you're with George. I wanted to tell you that if George were to stay overnight it's alright with me." Instead, you might want to say, "I wanted to tell you I appreciate your not having George here overnight when I'm home as it would make me feel very uncomfortable." Your mother then knows where you stand and it can help her in her decisions, which are very personal and private ones.

Remarriage

Many parents do remarry and many form common-law unions — that is, a couple live together as husband and wife without a legal marriage. This often occurs with separations as one partner may be waiting for divorce proceedings to be completed or not wanting to go through the divorce because of the expense. For our purpose, I am going to refer to all these new unions as remarriages.

In the group, one in every two people had one or both parents remarried. One in every four people had one or both parents currently living in a common-law marriage. Parents remarried from one to five years, with an average of three and one quarter years, following the initial separation. Common-law unions tended to come immediately or within one year after the first separation. Only one in twelve people in the group had both parents remarried.

Should parents include their children or ask their teenagers if they are planning to remarry? Duncan says it's good to ask: "My mother remarried. She asked everybody and we all agreed. He's a really great guy." Gordon disagrees: "Just do it. It's their own choice. I wouldn't ask for permission if I wanted to marry, why should they? I wouldn't feel I had any right to disapprove." If your parents contemplate a second union you may find yourself fearing that it, too, will break up. Bev notes, "Kids fear that they will split up again. I hope my parents will make sure that this is going to work."

You may find yourself invited to your parent's wedding. Should you go? This appears to be a very individual decision. There was no consensus of opinion among the people I spoke with. Some expressed their disapproval of the marriage by refusing to attend. Marion was a bit miffed that she was not given a chance to refuse: "I didn't get an invitation. My sister did. I didn't get the satisfaction of saying, 'No thanks.' I don't agree with what he did. I might be exaggerating but I don't condone it." But others, like Elizabeth, were glad to be asked: "I wanted to share in his happiness. It's always been a fear of mine that he wouldn't want me. My dad asked me about his remarriage. I'd feel awful if he left me out."

What kind of feelings are likely to emerge as you contemplate a parent's remarriage? Jeff says, "I'd like to see my father get married again but my mother doesn't need it. He needs someone to be dependent upon." Many people were concerned that their parents had not yet resolved their personal problems arising out of the first marriage before entering another. One such case is that of Marion's father: "Yes, I think he's trying to start over again, but you can't at 45 or 50. He's going to have a lot of guilt feelings and self-evaluation because his relationship with his new wife is going the same way. He's going to fall on his face. My mother will be alone when she's older and I wish she'd get remarried then." This was a common feeling expressed by the group. It is difficult to leave home and start out on your own, if you're left with the feeling you're deserting your mother or father. Your parent, however, may prefer to be alone rather than to enter into a marriage of convenience.

Some people felt they would prefer to see their parents legally divorced and remarried than to continue in a common-law union. Barry feels his father has not arranged for a legal divorce because of the financial entanglements. "He had a fake wedding — he and his girlfriend, because my parents weren't legally divorced.

A ceremony and everything. I wasn't there. His girlfriend's daughter, she believes that they're legally married. I guess it was a very realistic wedding. He's pretty stupid. I'd rather see them legally married, my parents divorced and my mother getting the proper alimony. It makes me want to ruin it for them but I haven't got the guts."

Once your father or mother has remarried, it may seem very strange to go and visit. This may be especially hard if your parent's new wife or husband has children. You will feel a little out of place with your new step-brothers or step-sisters. Abby: "Right now, when I go to my dad's house, I feel a bit awkward because there's him and his wife and my sister and my step-sister and they're very close and I feel in the middle and I've had a really hard time with my step-mother because, at first, I saw her as a threat trying to replace my mother. In some ways she is like my mother and in other ways she definitely isn't and it's those other ways that I blame her for. I think she's wrong and a lot of the times I feel guilty because I go to my dad's house and if I do get along with her — my dad's wife — then I feel badly if my mum knows that and a lot of the fights that my parents have, my step-mother knows about them, and I keep saying to myself that obviously she would take my father's side because she sees him getting very upset at my mother at what they talked about, what they yelled about and often she will say things. She said about three things in the last few years about my mother, remarks that came out which were really uncalled for because they're criticisms about my mom. She said that I remind her of my mom, that it's not me, it's my mother who's talking and really it brings out all the hard feelings that she actually has about my mother and that's hard to deal with. You've got to remember that when your parents start going out the person they're going out with is just an ordinary human being and has affection for one of your parents but it's not an actual threat. They're not trying to replace the parent, but trying to replace mother and father. They might have come through a divorce themselves. I had so many prejudgments. But I know you have to start from scratch. Her position is difficult too. I used to have terrible feelings about my step-mother when I first started going over there, and I didn't even know her. I think it takes a long time. I think you have to be a certain age."

When we were younger we all read in stories and fairy tales about evil step-mothers. I guess it's only natural to be a bit apprehensive. As Abby points out, she has to get to know you and it's a difficult situation for her as well. The first time Richard went to his father's new house, he found that his father tended to favor him while his step-mother favored her children a bit: "But she tries also to be nice to me because she realized that, at first, I hated her. It was strange, meeting after the marriage. I didn't have anything to say — all the initiative came from her. She's really nice. But I wouldn't tell Mom that. Mom hated the idea of me liking his new wife."

Indeed, in the situation of remarriage, you have to be very careful to let your parents know that you love them both and that they will always be your parents. A step-parent can become close to you and be well-liked by you without being a replacement for your parent. Still, some of the teenagers I spoke with felt that they didn't want to get to know this new person at all. Unfortunately, refusal to meet the new marriage partner can endanger your relationship with your parent. This is the kind of situation that Marion is in:

"I'm worried that she'll end up like my mother. I didn't get involved with my father's new wife because that's my personal protest. I didn't approve and I didn't really want to bother myself with that. I just thought it would be hard on me to see my father with another lady and I still think I'm right in a way. My father is constantly pressuring me to see her and I keep telling him I don't want to and that is severing the relationship between my father and myself which I don't want. But it's not my fault because every single time I talk to him it's always, 'Well I can't go out to dinner with you because you won't let her come along.' Well, that hurts because I'm his daughter. That sort of says to me that he never really cared. I also realize he feels very guilty for what he's done, which doesn't help us."

Marion seems to be paying quite a price for her "personal protest". But she's not alone: Annette has the same conviction: "All of us, like my brothers and I, we are jealous of my dad's wife. My dad is remarried and he has kids. Whenever I see my father I like to see him alone because I don't like being with her. It's not that I don't like her as a person but I don't like the way she could, I don't like the way anybody could be with someone else who's married at that point." While I respect Marion's and Annette's moral values, I fear that these same values might cause a further distancing from their fathers.

Jim has both a new step-father and a new step-mother. He says, "A step-parent can't replace a parent. My mother is afraid her husband's kids might think she wanted to be their mother, but she's just there to be this guy's wife. I wouldn't want my father's new wife to be a replacement. When my step-mother's family comes over I'm included too."

Most of these situations, as with most of the

group, are remarriages of fathers. In our group three out of four remarriages were fathers with new wives. But some people did have step-fathers or common-law partners living in their home. Although most people found they missed the discipline of a two-parent family, they very much resented a step-parent making or enforcing rules in the home. You may find this, particularly in the case of a step-father. It is only natural for a mother who is having a small argument with her adolescent son to turn to her adult male partner for assistance. You may find yourself being very resentful if your step-father comes to your mother's defence.

Jerry feels this anger might have something to do with feeling competitive: "Last year my mother married again to another guy. He has three children. Once in a while I feel competitive with him. It doesn't really bother me. I get along fine with him but one thing that bothers me is having to tell people, 'Oh, my parents are divorced and my mother is married to somebody else and he has three children.' It seems really strange to me." The same reaction to a step-father moving into the area of discipline can also affect girls. Sally found this: "Last March my mother was going out with a guy with four kids. Mom and he decided to buy a house. He decided he'd be fatherly. I'd back off and be a little brat. It just didn't work out. They realized what they'd done wrong. Everybody has a different way of living."

I don't want to give you the wrong impression. Not everyone whose parent or parents remarried encountered great difficulties, but everyone did find that some adjustment was necessary. It takes time to get to know the new marriage partner. Time also to establish new routines, not impose old ones on a new situation. Your step-parent will need your help through open communication about what you appreciate and what you find offensive. If there is no give and take, no mutual co-operation, of course it won't work. You may still find yourself faced with painful choices but some of these changes may, as with Nancy's father, have a positive outcome: "I didn't want him to get married but now I've got to know his girlfriend I don't mind the idea. She really cares about me a lot. I gained a lot through his girlfriend. She woke my dad up and he changed. I lost a little the relationship with my mother when I first became close with Dad's girlfriend but everything's fine now."

You may find yourself with a number of new step-brothers and step-sisters. Jim has his own brother, two sisters and a brother from his mother's remarriage and two brothers from his father's remarriage. He finds he gets along well with the step-brother and step-sisters with whom he's living, but he finds his father's wife's children to be too immature — just not his type.

Being the same age as your parents' new step-children can make you feel quite jealous. If you are not living with your father and he has a new step-son or step-daughter your age, you may resent the amount of time he has for them and how little time he has to be with you. Even if you understand how important it is for this new situation to work out and even if you want your father to be happy, it can sometimes be painful. Annette feels this way when she sees the reaction of her younger brother. Her father has a step-son the same age: "My brother gets jealous 'cause he doesn't have his father. Nobody is able to spend time with him, especially when he's the same age. I know it's his family and a new life, a new beginning. I'm glad he's happy." Perhaps Annette's father thinks he's giving both boys a good time by bringing them together and in some cases he might be right. Here it might help if Annette or her brother told their father of their feelings. He would then understand that they are not angry or rejecting their step-brother but need more time to adjust. Perhaps they could go out alone with their father once in a while until they are more comfortable.

What if your parent and his or her new partner have children of their own? Elizabeth worries that she'll be left out: "I'm afraid that they'll start a new family. I'll be accepted second. I'm kind of scared if he had a child from his present wife that the kid would be cherished more." This is a perfectly normal worry, even for people whose parents aren't divorced — that a younger child will be more loved. But a strange phenomenon of human nature is that parents can have more children and love them as well. Parents sometimes worry about the same thing — they fear having another child because they love the first one and think it will take away from the first to have a second. When the second child is born they are surprised that they still love the first one — and the second one as well. It is a mistake to think of love as if it could be measured. We say that because a parent has less time available for us, therefore, he or she loves us less. But the love exists even though the parent can't be with us. It is not a fixed quantity of which only so much is available. I feel this is important to remember, not only in the case of your parent starting a new family but also in the event that a parent moves away. Although there is a great distance between you, the affection still survives.

ADVICE ON DATING:

For adolescents

1 Your parent will date when he or she wants to. Don't push!
2 Don't become too involved with your parent's dates early on.
3 If bringing dates home for the night offends you, let your parent know. Be diplomatic — *Their* sex life is not really *your* concern.

For parents

1 Date if you want to. Your teenagers will not be as distressed as younger children.
2 Bring your kids and your friend's children together only after you're sure of the relationship.
3 Don't bring your dates home for the night or the weekend until you've talked it over with your children. It's not your sexual life they're concerned with, but having a stranger at the breakfast table. Don't surprise them.

ADVICE ON REMARRIAGE:

For adolescents

1 Even if you don't approve of a remarriage, don't lose contact with your parent.
2 Give your step-parent time to adjust before you judge him or her.

For parents

1 A steady boyfriend or girlfriend or a common-law relationship coming too soon after the separation can be distressing for the children. They feel re-

      jected. *Reassure* them.

2   Spend some time with your own children alone, separate from your new partner and step-children. They need to know you still care for them.

3   Don't expect your spouse to become your child's parent, and don't expect your teenager to accept your spouse as a parent.

10
On Getting Help.

Who can you go to for help, support and understanding? Forty-one percent of the adolescents in the group found their parents to be most helpful, with friends (34%) and other relatives (23%) being seen as people more likely to be of assistance than psychologists, psychiatrists or marriage counsellors (15%). Teachers were seen as helpful by only five percent of the group. Of course, no one can fully understand what you are going through and what it has been like for you. Only you know that.

Parents

Some people found their parents understood some but not all of what they had experienced. Marion says, "My mother knows it's been hard for me but not in what ways. It doesn't matter that much." Bob found that talking with his parents many times led to more of an understanding: "My parents understood a lot of things

I experienced. We talked about it as a sort of common theme for months afterward."

It would be unrealistic to expect an angry parent to put away his or her biases and sit down and calmly talk about such an emotionally charged subject. It's not surprising that many in the group found their parents to be helpful in some areas but to have blind spots in other areas. Abby found this: "My mother knows that I've assumed much more responsibility. She understands that I've had a hard time adjusting to the relationship between both her and my step-mother. My dad doesn't realize. He says he realizes how difficult it was for me but I guess he doesn't realize or my mom doesn't realize about the people they go out with and also about trying to be neutral. My mom encouraged me to talk to someone and to look at my problems objectively."

Of course, the parent who is at home is more available and may, therefore, seem more concerned. Barbara appreciated this kind of support even though she did not feel her parents could understand: "My dad was out of the home so it was hard for him to understand. My mother was just angry. I felt they weren't feeling what I was feeling. But she was there when I needed her." Similarly, Margaret realizes her mother has her own burdens, but Margaret appreciates her mother's efforts: "My mother does a little but my father doesn't know what I've gone through. Financially and materially my mother's been there to raise me but that's it. She's concerned about herself and her career. She had to go to work full-time to support us."

Boys who are living with their mothers may find not having a father to confide in difficult. Michael's mother recognized this but didn't fully understand: "Well, at times she would ask if I felt a need for male advice and suggest I go to see my uncles or cousins. But she didn't really understand I wanted a father-son relationship." Joel also had some problems living with his mother: "My parents understood and really tried to help me. My father told me to keep calm and try and help my sister. He gave me money to get flowers for Mom on Mother's Day even though he hates my mother. But my mother doesn't help as much because I've grown like my father in many ways and that scares her."

On the other hand, Jerry, who lives with his father and three brothers, finds it difficult to get his mother to understand. I like his suggestion that helping is a two-way street of being listened to and understood but having to be willing to listen in return: "One thing a guy has to do if his parents are getting a divorce is he still needs a lot of support from his parents and the parents need a lot of support from the child. I gave my father a lot of support. The only thing I ever got from my mother is not really very helpful. She says that she knows how hard it must be for me to live with my father. I don't believe she just says that right out! It's gross. My mother just cares for herself — my father helps me through. He's given me advice on how to go through life."

While parents like Duncan's would be ideal, "they don't fully understand, but enough that they help out more. Both my parents are willing to talk with me any time." Not every parent has the capacity or the personality to sit down and talk things out. You may find that one parent says he or she cares by doing things with you, as does Jim's mother: "My dad understands now. My mother appreciates us going through it — she's glad we got through it okay. They're both supportive in different ways. My mom wants me to come on trips with them as a family and that's okay. Dad helps more as a person. He encourages me."

If you want your parents to understand, you must begin by letting them know what you need. If you want to talk more, you may have to spell it out. If you want to do more things together, you may have to bluntly say so. Barry says, "My mother completely understands. She's gotten me over it. My father hasn't done much. He would say it's because I just wouldn't let him." Maybe Barry's father is right. Even the most well-intentioned parent needs direction on how to be helpful.

Friends

Younger children are sometimes embarrassed to tell their friends about separation or divorce. To them, it's admitting that their parents don't care about them and that they must have done something wrong. It is unlikely that you, as an adolescent, will feel that you're at fault for your parents' separation, but you may still feel awkward about sharing with your friends. Jerry was anxious at first about what to say to his friends: "I figured I had to go to school — but what was I going to tell my friends? You know they're going to find out. I felt kind of embarrassment. I didn't tell anybody for a couple of days. Then one day I met a friend outside the schoolyard, I guess we were talking about divorce or something. His parents were having problems, too. I just told him what happened. He didn't believe it but all he said was, 'I'm sorry for you.' So from my good friend it happened to go around and a lot of people found out. A lot of people came up and asked me about it. I just told them what happened — I didn't tell anybody why. I hang around with about six kids, and four of them have divorced parents. Divorced kids are actually very spoiled, just like you see in the movies. I think I'm the same as before. It's been so long now, if anybody comes up to me I just say, 'My parents are divorced.' "

Jeff found it hard to talk initially, although he didn't mind people knowing: "The first time I ever told anybody that my parents had actually separated was my best friend. I think it was on the night when my mother came over to take some stuff away and he was over there. We were just hanging around and I told him. It's very embarrassing. It's a hard thing to say because it does take a while to actually get used to it. My mother was a teacher at my school and my sister's school so word got around pretty fast. I was never really embarrassed by it; I just didn't want to talk about it too much. But now I talk with my friends."

It seems that once one gets over the initial barrier it's much easier to tell friends. Bob feels that it may be gratifying to tell people: "Well, it's fairly common these days so I think it isn't anything to be embarrassed about. In fact, anyone can go through the separation of their parents — in a kind of funny way, it's a modern status symbol."

But when should you tell your friends? What should you tell them? Most people start by telling one close friend whom they trust and feel will respect their confidence. Bev recalls, "At first, I was sort of reluctant to tell my friends about it, but I told my best friend. She understood and promised not to tell any of my other friends, so I just told her. I wasn't ashamed of it — it's just that it made me sad when I thought about it. But I didn't tell any of my friends he (my father) was an alcoholic because I was sort of ashamed that he was one." Barbara felt the same way in trying to explain to her friends about alcoholism: "At first I just told them they were separated and the questions were asked: 'Why?' 'My dad's an alcoholic.' They didn't even know what that means so I became more quiet. But I'm a lot more open now." Judging from Bev and Barbara's experience, you might want to be prepared to answer the question, "Why?". Joel feels that a simple clear explanation of the truth clears the air and allows you to relate more directly with your friends: "I tell them my parents split up and how I feel. I just say the truth and then get off the subject because they feel sorry and don't know what to say." Abby agrees that getting things out into the open allows you to relate more naturally: "When I was going through it, all my school friends' parents were together. Now I find about three-quarters of my classes, people come from separated or divorced families. At first, though, I was embarrassed about it and it was kind of awkward. I'm glad I told them because now I don't feel I'm hiding something. I don't just walk up and tell them, but I explain the way I feel."

So many people reported that now a lot of their friends' parents are divorced too that I began to wonder if the rising divorce rate alone could account for this. I wondered if the adolescents in the group didn't change their friends after their parents' separations. Is it easier to get close to people who have had the same experience as you have? I asked the group if their friendships had changed afterwards. Jim says he is definitely more attracted to people whose parents are divorced: "When

I moved to an apartment there were lots of kids from divorced families. I started hanging out with these guys. They aren't stupid like people who's parents are together. I think we are more mature. But I got into a bit of crime. You learn from your mistakes."

I hope Jim is not implying that "people who are from broken homes get into trouble." One often hears that said, and it can happen, if you're angry or hurt, that you'll take your anger out through getting into delinquent activities. But this doesn't mean that *all* people whose parents are separated become criminals. However, Joel does caution us about the choice of friends: "I began to pick bad friends. I picked one bad friend. (I should say most of my friends were good.) Towards last Christmas this bad friend and I stole $15.00 from my sister and went to a sports shop and purchased pellet guns. We were caught, but my mother didn't know I kept the gun. It was kind of an extension of my hostility. Now I have better friends. I have two good friends who are in this situation right now. We talk it out. Another of my friends grew to hate his father and he still hates his father. I'm trying to get it through to him that you can't hate your parents. It helps me to help them somehow. I have another friend who has become really violent and he's gotten into drugs. That's what I could have become if I didn't talk it out. It's nice to get it off my chest."

Bev joined an organization that helps kids with single parents meet one another: "I met new friends through an organization for one-parent families. It helps, having friends who understand." Barbara babysits for the same organization and finds that through helping younger children she's helped herself: "I've babysat a lot of 10 and 11-year-old kids whose parents are divorced. I can be up with them to 2:00 in the morning listening to their problems. I mean it's sort of the blind leading the blind. It's just hard to understand, but talking it out helps."

Don't be disappointed if some friends find it hard to know how to respond at first. Marion wasn't discouraged that she didn't get the response she expected from her boyfriend, because she trusted that someone else would understand: "I told my boyfriend first of all, but I wasn't satisfied with the reaction because, you know, he didn't know what to do or say and I felt that it was useless, and it's like that with a lot of people. Well, I know he cared but it's just like telling him the daily news — you don't get any comfort from the response. On the other hand, I have a fantastic girlfriend. She's been my really super close friend ever since Grade 2. I thank God for her because when I told her she cried and I cried and we hugged each other. It was wonderful. That was the only person who ever really helped me just by showing that emotion. I think you have to be careful who you tell. I went through a stage where I was telling almost everyone I met that my parents were divorced, because I was looking for pity."

Laurie got caught up in telling everyone about the divorce and she almost lost some of her friends: "My friends were very good through the whole thing. I'd go around and I was a real bitch all day. I was depressed. I wouldn't talk to anybody, or when I did all I did was talk about the divorce and what it was doing. I lost quite a few friends at the time without realizing it. Finally, my best friend came up and told me straight out to quit talking about it all the time. They were my friends and they were around when I needed help, but it wasn't a 48-hour-a-day job. At first I was really hurt when she told me this and I sulked even more and finally it hit me — what I was doing to myself and to my friends. I wasn't their friend anymore. They were just a leaning post for me to talk to. They were pretty good. They were understanding. They spent time with me and tried to keep me out of the house as much as possible."

Friends who know about the separation can be helpful in giving advice as well as listening. Margaret's girlfriend, who understood, was able to get her started in a whole new direction. "My best friend's parents split up when we were in Grade 5. About four or five years later it happened to me. I went to her and I talked to her a lot. I stayed overnight a few times. She really advised me, sort of talked to me about it and gave me security. She told me how to respond. I was very lucky to have her. She even helped me talk to my mother. She got me really sort of self-confident. Before the separation I was a real mess — a tom-boy in torn jeans and dirty T-shirts. Now I don't go out of the house without sort of dressing decently and thinking highly of myself." Richard finds he has not changed his friends, but the ones he had have become much closer and this helps him greatly: "I guess I tend to make closer friends. Like, the friends I do have are really quite close. I go over to their house almost all the time. This way I think I compensate for the loss that I never realized I had up until just lately."

Richard speaks of going over to his friend's house and getting a warm feeling from being there. What kind of reaction can you expect from friends' parents to the news that your parents are separated? Most people found that they reacted kindly but didn't get too involved. Jim got a mixed reaction: "Some were helpful and some thought I was a criminal." So some negative attitudes about "kids from broken homes" still persist.

Both Elizabeth and Sally came into contact with prejudiced adults but found that they could ignore it when they had good, trusted friends. Elizabeth says: "The school I was in was very middle-class. The parents did not want their children to associate with separated children — kids from broken homes — I'd give them bad ideas. 'That's not the right thing to do.' Their noses would be turned up: 'She had problems in her family — my mother doesn't want me to get close to her.' I kept my distance. It made me angry, but I had good friends to fall back on." Sally recalls, "In the neighborhood, divorce was a really bad thing. So they didn't actually say unhelpful things but they looked at me and said: 'Oh, you are the one with the divorced parents.' It kind of bugged me but I learned to ignore it."

I think you must trust that people will see you for what you are as a person. If friends' parents seem to want to help you by inviting you over for dinner or the evening, accept this as a kindness. Laurie was anxious that she would lose her friends as her mother suggested she might: "I kind of got adopted by a few families. It was really kind of nice. I was part of a family and I've always been close with my friends and their families. We've all got along very well and it was just a nice, general, happy family feeling. However, a few of my friends' parents felt that their children shouldn't associate with me because of the divorce. When one of my friends' parents got divorced in Grade 8 I was thinking, 'How will people react?' My mother said, 'Well they're wealthy. It's not going to make any difference. But in our case people would look down on you. You won't be as good as people. You don't have money. All your friends will drop you.' That's a pretty heavy load to lay on a kid. I guess I started thinking of myself as inferior. But my friends weren't like that at all."

Michael recalls how important it was for him to have friends whose parents recognized his needs. "When I was younger — even before they separated, I think — it's a Jewish tradition on Friday night, they light candles and say a blessing over a glass of wine. Usually the father does it. My father didn't come home until late on a Friday night and we didn't do family things. I'd go to a friend's house and I would be there with their family. It was nice because it was a tradition. I was glad that they shared it with me. I suppose they recognized the situation and were willing to share a bit of their family with me. It's really nice when a family friend recognizes that kind of need and steps in to help out."

Relatives

Grandparents are in a very difficult position. Staying neutral and continuing to see their grandchildren is made even harder if those grandchildren are living with their daughter-in-law or son-in-law. Remaining close to their grandchildren can be interpreted as not supporting their own son or daughter. So grandparents stand to lose the family most readily in a divorce: most people I spoke with saw their grandparents from both sides of the family less frequently after the separation. This may simply be part of growing up. Jill, however, found that her grandparents on both sides were helpful: "My father's mother was relieved when they broke up. She's been really supportive and wanted to keep a good relationship despite the divorce. My mother's mother was also supportive. She sought me out a lot. It's worn off a bit over the years but she's always there if I need her — I'm just too busy."

Laurie and her grandmother were less fortunate: "My maternal grandfather was happy I went with my mother — otherwise he would have disowned me. My paternal grandmother was sorry about it. But when she sort of stuck with my father I held it against her. Now I'm sorry for it." Not all relatives can remain caring and understanding, but if they do you will probably want to try to keep in contact with them. Sometimes, as with Sally, if you continue to see a grandparent, even though they may not understand at first, he or she will come around, given time: "My father's mother was sort of on my dad's side at first and she thought Mom was the culprit. But now she sees all of us. She used to think I was a brat but now she understands."

Counsellors

"The anger seemed to be spreading out and it was like a volcano in me that was fuel slowly building up and when it finally erupted and that's when finally my second oldest brother told my mom to get help for me," Barbara states. "I needed it. I thought that the help was because of the anger of my mom having a boyfriend. I mean, it just seemed everything was building up and I didn't understand why. It wasn't happening to anyone else that I know of and that made me angrier because here, once again, another sort of, like, black mark against me. So, finally I went to see a psychologist. She was very good for me. This was a few years ago now, when things were at their worst and I saw her and she helped me. I found out a lot of my problems stemmed from way back. Like, from being over-sensitive because of having to wear braces, because I had buck teeth and was called Beaver and just a lot of things that way. I was burying myself in T.V. I was running away from life. Then the psychologist helped me. It seemed that it was really Mom's boyfriend I hated because he was taking the place of my father. It didn't make any sense to me. I wouldn't accept it. I wanted to blame everyone. But the doctor helped me realize you just can't blame them — that it was me that this anger was sprouting from. I was mad 'cause it was Mom's boyfriend who was taking us places and things and my dad never did. It was the resentment and jealousy of my mom being taken away from me that I couldn't accept. By the end of the year — I'd been going every week to see the psychologist — it helped me realize that the divorce had affected me a lot more than I thought. I thought it was an inconvenience. Just another black mark of sort of taking me out of a group and putting me by myself. When I realized what I was doing I felt upset. After a year the situation got better. Like, sure there's a few problems now, but I mean that's only to be expected."

Some of the people I spoke with had been to family counsellors with their parents before the separation, and others went by themselves with one parent afterwards. Three families went once or twice for some counselling before the first separation. Most were only invited to two or three sessions, although Richard went ten times. Generally, people in the group felt that although it didn't work for their family it might for another. Jeff explains what happened in their family counselling: "Before the divorce, my parents got into the psychiatric thing. We went to a place where we all sat down and all tried to figure out the problems. But I never felt easy talking to the people. When I see a big mirror on the wall, knowing that there are five other people looking at us, recording what we're doing and everybody knows about it — you know, it's good that they're trying to help but it's hard to talk knowing that they are all there. Also, it's difficult trying to express your feelings with others around. What you say could actually hurt them."

Richard, who had the most counselling prior to the separation, was not clear about the underlying reasons for going: "I first became aware of problems through counselling. I was only 12. It was before the separation. Our family went together for treatment — we had six sessions. Well, at first we had six basic sessions. We went for a total of 9 or 10. I think Mom felt we were having problems at home. I think she also felt she was having a marital problem. I didn't understand at the time. I thought it was just because of my older brother who had been causing a little static in the house but over a year later I realized what had been going on." Sally feels that she couldn't recommend family counselling because, in her family, it caused more problems: "When I was 12 my parents told my brother and I that they were getting separated. Right on my birthday, when I turned 12. There was a lot of screaming and everything. My mother told us that we would go to a marriage counsellor, our whole family. My father refused, so my brother, my mother and I came down to the city and visited the marriage counsellor. He told us to force my father to go and we did but it didn't seem to help any. My father was going to be stubborn and irrational about the whole thing. It created problems because they forced us to tell Dad we were scared of him — but it did show us how to cope."

What about counselling after the separation for you alone? Usually this type of counselling is confidential, but this depends on the law where you live and how old you are. In some places the records of what you say to a counsellor can be subpoenaed and used in court. If you are considering seeing a counsellor, you will want to discuss confidentiality with him or her before you begin so you know what your rights are and whether or not he or she will be discussing things with your parents. In some areas of the country your parents have to give written permission for you to attend.

Eight people in the group I spoke with had seen their own counsellors. These adolescents went for regular weekly appointments for three months to two years after the separation: most of them had counselling for about six months. Some, like Jerry and Margaret, didn't like the counselling and stopped immediately. Margaret says, "It didn't help at all so I didn't go again. You should go once and find out. If it helps, go, but if it doesn't, you can't say you never tried." For Jerry it was slightly different. He was forced to see a psychiatrist: "I didn't want to go at all — court ordered it. It added hate towards my mother because it was all her doing. She wanted custody and her lawyer would try and do these things. No go. I don't think I needed it."

It seems better if you want to seek some counselling that you go on your own to someone of your own choice. Remember that you don't have to continue with the first counsellor you meet. Counsellors understand that it may be easier to talk to one kind of person rather than another. A counsellor will not be offended if you say, for example, that you would rather talk to a man than a woman or that you would prefer someone who listens more than someone who gives advice. A good counsellor will help you find the right person for you to talk with. Although John did not agree with the psychiatrist he saw, he feels that the counsellor may have something to offer other people: "After they separated there was my father and me against my mom, and there was my mom and father against me. It was really unusual. I went to a psychiatrist and I was given various theories about it. Before my father and I were so close but it was kind of fake. The psychiatrist — it's kind of a strange theory — told me that my father was trying to live out his life through me. Like, he had a lousy childhood and he was on my hockey team. He was always playing football with me in the backyard. But, like, the way I saw it then and the way I still think is that we were just real close. It wasn't formal. I was going with this girl and her father's a psychiatrist. It was free, whenever I wanted to go. It's a good idea."

Jill seems to think that, besides helping her understand the separation and her feelings about it, her counselling sessions helped in other ways: "My dad scoffed when I started seeing a psychologist just before he left. It was just a little while before he left. Mainly I went for contraceptives, but it turned into a counselling sort of routine and I'd go every couple of weeks and just talk to a woman who was just fantastic. I'd just talk and talk and talk because my mother was so preoccupied with the whole separation bit and the whole marriage breakup bit that I just could not talk to her at all. This also happened to be at a period in time when I didn't have any friends really. I was very lonely. It helped me amazingly. By the time I finished, Dad had left and I had friends and was getting involved at school. My marks went shooting up and I was really happy. I've never felt the need to talk to anyone anymore."

School

Having difficulties in the family can affect your school work. It's hard to concentrate if your mind is wandering home to the problems there. Not everyone found that their school work suffered greatly, but the people who did found it to be a temporary situation. What happened to Jim is not unusual: "For a while, just for a year, my marks went down. I didn't fail or anything but I used to get A's and things in early grades but then I missed too much school in moving around and things. Ever since then I've been getting A's in some subjects." Jeff says: "You sit down to study and it's always on your mind."

Some of the group, however found that the release of tension at home and the end of the uncertainty helped, so that their marks improved. Abby says: "My marks improved. I spend more time on my work." Jill compensated for her feelings about the separation by "throwing myself into my school work."

Ted feels that his school work has suffered for years because of the situation at home. "My father's an alcoholic. My parents have been divorced for three or four years. Now I'm 18, but when I was 8 or so I began having problems in school which have passed on through the years. In fact, I'm still having problems in school because of that. You go to school at 9 o'clock in the morning but you've been up the night earlier until 3:00 and 4:00 in the morning because your father was screaming and yelling or just keeping you up, so you're going to school very tired in the morning. This problem went on until I was 13 and my parents started separating. It's getting better in school." This raised the question as to whether it would have helped if the teachers had been aware of Ted's difficulties. Should you let the school know about problems at home?

Most people I spoke with said that the school finds out eventually because of forms that you have to fill in the first day of classes each year. Some people felt it would be good if the teacher knew because if you were drifting off in class they might understand better. Other people felt that it would be helpful if the principal, but not the teachers, knew. Jim wanted understanding, not favoritism: "I used to get pity marks from teachers. They felt sorry for me. When my parents got a divorce not everybody was like today. It was 'Wow! Their parents are divorced', you know. Something really different. Next year I had a teacher who was a pretty nice guy. He understood about divorce but he didn't give me pity marks. I got my marks up. We moved and I went to a new school. The school I went to before was a Catholic school and they didn't like the idea of my parents separating. I'm glad I'm not at the school anymore because I don't like the religion. This year I'm fooling around too much at school and losing my credits. I'm skipping too much school and things like that, but it has nothing to do with the divorce. I would advise people to go and get help from a friend but never from the school. They think they understand so much but they don't."

Jim's opinion is a minority one. Although most of the adolescents said they hadn't gone to a guidance counsellor or a teacher at school, they felt that these people might be useful to someone else.

It seems strange that more people don't approach their teachers. John explains how helpful one of his teachers was: "I just sort of had things building up inside of me and I was getting really hostile. Lately I've been talking to people. There's this English teacher. He's just an exceptional person because he wasn't your standard English teacher. He was at an alternative school and he'd left. I'd really gotten along with him well and I talked to him. He's been having his own personal problems lately so he's been really decent. We've just sort of gotten along together. You've got to talk it out. You get so much hostility built into you just like your parents do. You begin to get paranoid and it isn't too good."

Elizabeth also found her teachers a great help: "When they first separated I switched schools. My new Grade 8 teacher was like a second father to me. If I stayed off school he'd just talk to me about life. In Grade 8 I was a terrible mess. I found a note my mother left for the teacher. It said my mom was having trouble with me. I was angry at the world. I had to look out for me. The teacher asked me out for lunch. My teachers have just been great. I wanted someone who knew me to help me out, not some social worker. My Grade 11 teacher noticed if I was troubled and he'd take me out and we'd talk about it. If parents are forcing a psychiatrist or a social worker upon you, I don't believe in that. Get an outside view from a teacher. They are like good friends. It could be a neighbor. You need male support. I always reached out to males and this worried me. I found it better to talk to a male teacher than boyfriends."

Are there special courses at school in health or family studies that might help you understand various aspects of divorce better? Some people told me of some courses like this, but they found that academic courses weren't as good as group discussion or drama. Drama seems to be a good course if you want to learn to express yourself more openly. Margaret, Michael and Jill all exercised another option. They found that after their parents' separation the regular academic program was too restrictive for them. They chose an alternate school program with more responsibility for the individual student. This seemed to fit with their developing maturity in other areas as well. Margaret says: "I was going to school but finally at the end of Term One at school I couldn't take it anymore. I was going to school where they had strict courses and exams and tests and really hard things and just sort of normal school routines. I couldn't take it. So I switched schools and I went to a much better school and I'm really enjoying it. They offer a lot of courses, you know, millions of courses and they're only one term long. Before, I used to get up in the morning with a 'Oh no, what's going to happen today? Am I going to pass out at school? Am I going to freak out in the street? What's going to happen?' Now I'm at the new school, it just changed my whole outlook. The people at my old school knew everything about my parents. I came to school one day with a bruise on my arm. And everyone was asking me, 'What happened?' I said I had a fight with my brother and he hit me. They somehow found out that my father hit me and it was all over the school. I just couldn't take it anymore. They started feeling really sorry for me and pitying me and it was really bad. I couldn't handle it anymore and there were rumors going around. I was on the outside and I was rejected. Don't ever believe that garbage that you're never an outsider and never rejected if your parents separate. But I've become a completely and totally better person as a result of it. I enrolled in a course in psychology and I'm doing fabulously. I got Honors and everything last term."

I'm certainly not saying that an alternate school or a different course would be helpful to everyone. What I would like to suggest is that you seriously consider in what ways your school might be helpful to you.

ADVICE ON GETTING HELP:

For adolescents
1   Help your parents to understand you. Talk to them.
2   Tell your friends, but don't burden them.
3   If at all possible, keep in touch with grandparents.
4   If you go for counselling, choose carefully and wisely.
5   Explore the resources at your school.

For parents
1   Organizations such as Parents without Partners, One Parent Families, Single Fathers and others can help you put your adolescent in touch with self-help groups.

11
Losses and Gains.

What are some of the changes you can expect as a result of your parents' separation? During the adolescent years many changes take place. I'm speaking not just of physical maturation but of such things as increased responsibility, decreasing parental discipline, friends and jobs. While these changes occur for every adolescent, many with whom I spoke felt that their parents' separation had had a real effect on their developing maturity. Some felt it resulted in their assuming a responsibility and mature attitude much earlier than they would have done otherwise.

"You learn how to take care of yourself. You're more mature than other people," says Duncan. "I don't need anyone to tell me what to do. I behave more responsibly. You learn how to be more disciplined. I can stay out to any time I want but I limit myself. I just don't feel good staying out all night. You miss not having parents asking you what time you'll be in."

Discipline or parental rules seem to be very important in determining whether or not an adolescent takes more responsibility. Like Duncan, most of the people in the group said that their parents were not as strict after the separation. Jerry says: "I did what I wanted to do. He was quite willing to let me do it. Before the divorce he was quite strict. He wouldn't allow any long hair. He wouldn't allow late nights. He wouldn't allow any swearing in the house. After the divorce, well, three guys living together in a house change quite a lot. I was allowed a lot more freedom. I have a lot more independence. This enabled me to grow more within myself. I am more mature. It takes a lot of strength not to abuse this. You're only hurting yourself if you do this." Jim feels very much the same way: "Since the divorce, I'm more independent than I used to be. I don't have to be dependent on my parents. My dad lets us have more freedom to do what we want — but we don't take advantage of it, we don't abuse it. I hate kids who are too dependent on their parents for allowance and dumb things like that. Usually my father's working and he trusts us."

Duncan adds that although he feels he is more mature, he missed a great deal through this loss of discipline. He even goes so far as to say that it feels like a loss of family life and parental caring: "I think the loss of discipline is a loss too. You know, sometimes when I go call on my friends to go to a party or something his father or mother is always sitting there: 'Where are you going? Who's the person you're going with?' They *always* say, 'What time are you coming home?' He says 12.30, his father says 11.30. It's always an hour earlier. We go out and it's kind of strange 'cause I can stay out as late as I want but I always feel like they're telling me, too. I kind of miss it."

One parent alone may have more difficulty in deciding what is an appropriate curfew. Elizabeth says:

"She (my mother) trusts me. If my father was still with my mother it would be a lot stricter." Some of the group found that a lack of curfew and deadlines was not always a good thing. Laurie feels that "I walked all over my mother. It's weird not having a deadline. All my friends did. At first, I thought it was really great — then you start to think. My father was the one who always wanted to know where I was going and when I was coming back. But I still go in and out pretty well when I want to. Very few of my friends had this kind of freedom and I thought their parents were too strict. But with the divorce I kind of thought about it, like my mother should take more of an interest. I made up wild stories where I had been to get a reaction out of her." Gordon thinks that this lack of discipline came too soon, before he had time to learn patterns for self-discipline: "My parents let me do whatever I wanted — maybe they gave me too much freedom. It seemed to be a bit of indifference. At the time I thought it was great but now I'm sloppy and undisciplined with no regular system."

Before I talked to the adolescents in the group it seemed to me that a parent who was no longer in conflict with the other parent would be able to organize the house the way he or she wanted it. I had assumed that there would be more rules and discipline after the separation than before. Only Jill, who is living alone with her mother, found this to be the situation: "My mother's a little bit more protective. We have a lot of dicussions before I do something. He (my father) was very liberal."

I wondered why parents tend to be much more lenient after a separation. It may be that preoccupation with their own problems, such as moving and setting up a new household or adjusting to a new job, takes up most of their energy. Your parent may just be too drained to worry all the time where you are and what you're doing. If this happens, you may have to rely on the guidelines of your friends' parents, as Duncan did. You may have to set curfews and deadlines for yourself.

Many people found that the parent they were living with was forced to move fairly shortly after the separation. Such a move was generally made for financial reasons, but also sometimes to avoid painful memories. Annette recalls: "We moved from a village with a private pool to more compact housing because of the divorce — we couldn't afford it and Mother wanted to get away from the memories." Moving involves the loss not only of the home you had but also of friends and neighbors. Sometimes moving from a house to an apartment can be a difficult adjustment. Several adolescents were sad at having to give up their pets. Jim says: "A couple of months after Mom left we had to move from a big house with a lot of land in with my uncle and his family. We lost our cats and dog." A tragic thing happened when Michael moved: "Immediately after, we moved from a house into an apartment. Our hamsters were left behind and they died. Mother was in such a rush. I was really angry at Dad for not noticing them."

Even if you don't have to move for financial reasons, there may be financial problems in the family. You may find yourself suddenly much more aware of the family's financial condition. Some people, like Ted, felt that the family was better off financially after the separation. Ted's father had, at times, spent the family money on alcohol and after he left, although there were still financial difficulties, there was more security. Most people found that there was less money available. As Abby remembers, "My parents didn't have a lot of money for a long, long time and then my dad started to get successful in his business and my parents split up. My mother was forced to go out to work and she didn't have a university education so that was pretty difficult and now my dad's pretty well off. The difference between the two houses and the way they live is hard to take."

Barbara recalls some very difficult times for her family: "Yes, she's had difficulties. Being older, I'm realizing what inflation really means. Different prices of gas, food, everyday things to survive. My dad isn't giving her any support for us kids, he never has, so my eyes are open to what she's going through. That's what's urging me on to get a summer job, so I can help, and also my mom will say, 'Come here, take some money and buy some milk after lunch.' I say 'No way,' I don't see why I can't go home for lunch. I've chopped things because I have realized the financial thing. Kids will say, 'Want to go to the show?' I'll say, 'No, because I don't have the money.' Other kids have attitudes like, 'Why don't you get it from your mom?' That's immature.

"We live in subsidized government housing and I found it very bad. I remember episodes where I could bring a lunch to school and a girlfriend would take a cookie and she'd drop it on the floor and I would nearly be in tears because it was a waste. Because I knew the value of money because of the position where Dad had spent all our money and Mom was finding it hard and the only way she could see that we were going to make it was by her getting out on her own. In that way she would be bringing in the money herself."

You may find that not only are you more aware of the finances in the household but also you are more willing to help out by getting a job and paying for your own activities. John feels this way: "I used to get everything I wanted. I just had to ask. Now I work for what I want." Michael works setting up electronic equipment for concerts: "I'm expected to save my earnings for my education. I recognized that I have to support myself. I work about eight hours a week. It gives me a good feeling to have financial independence." Not everyone felt so positively about pitching in financially. At first, Laurie was quite ambivalent about working for the family: "My mom got stuck paying for my father's bankruptcy, and I guess she's owing now about $20,000. It was pretty hard for her. She made less than half my father's salary. So I got a job and my oldest brother got a job. I gave as much of my pay as I could to help around the house. I kind of resented it at first. I'm making this money so why am I giving it to my mom when I could be spending it? But then, once I thought about it, I figured I had a lot of time. She's got to have these payments. After a while I felt more mature and said, 'At least I can help out now.' It was a good feeling inside. It's pretty good at the end of the week to get a pay cheque and know you've earned it." Marion found that she not only had to help by using her own money, but her mother really needed her help in balancing the budget. "My mother was not experienced with finances. She needed more help. I have become familiar with every detail of our finances. I save my own money and pay for what I need."

Learning early in life about budgets and finances can be one of the real gains that comes out of the experience. It can be tough compared with other people your age, but Elizabeth points out some of the benefits for her: "I've learned to work for money, just through having to work. Most of my friends at school have $300 bonds. Well, I have never seen $300 in my bank account. They have bonds, they're driving expensive cars. I have come to learn to accept this. I say, 'That's them and I'm me.' In a sense I'm glad I'm not them. I've got all that much extra. I've got love. I've learned the wrongs and the rights in the world. I pay for school books, clothes, activities. I used to do housekeeping for a neighbor's. I didn't like that. She treated me like a kid who needed pocket money. Now I'm a clerk in a shop and I'm learning a lot."

Wanting to get a job may not be a direct result of your parents' separating. It may have to do with being more adult and more responsible. Richard's mother was very definite about his having to work but he might have wanted to get a job anyway: "There's always been pressure for me to get a job, even when I was 14. After I turned 16 it took me a couple of months to get a regular job. I work about 13 hours a week. My mother was on my back all the time but I was pretty lucky to get a job right away. I pay for my own clothes and everything." I wouldn't want to give the impression that everyone I spoke with had a job. Some people, like Michael, work very hard — 12 hours a week during the school year and 45 hours a week in the summer — but many people work only three hours a week at babysitting and some not at all. Duncan and Barry point out how working does give you a sense of contributing, even if you spend the money on yourself. Barry explains: "I have to work for extra things like concerts. That's good and I feel good about it. I don't really need to work. I just work for my own pleasure. But in a way you're helping the family not just living off your mother." Duncan says: "I work so I have my own money — then I don't mind if I spend it on something I want. I just work in the summer but I work in metal factories or loading trucks and I make plenty of money for the year.''

All work doesn't necessarily take place outside the home. The group found that after the separation mothers who had stayed home or worked part-time before tended to work full-time. This meant more household tasks had to be shared out. This was the way it was for Abby: "Since my mom has gone out to work and she likes everything very clean, when I come home from school 'til about 6 o'clock, I'm expected to do the vacuuming, cleaning, plus look after my sister 'til she comes home. My mom started working when my sister was in nursery, so when the bus drops her off I have to be there. Sometimes I resent it because I have things to do after school. I've accepted it pretty well. I didn't like the cleaning at first — now I just do it and get it done. Sometimes my mom will get a babysitter if I want to go out after school." Margaret also pitches in to help: "There's a lot of work which Dad didn't do around the house and now there's even more. My mother's constantly complaining. She's working full-time and there's a lot of things she can't do, so I do. I do the weekly shopping as well."

This may sound like a sexist remark, but it does seem that those families where there are three or four men living together find keeping the house running a real problem. Jerry finds that his mother is really missed: "She's not there to pamper you, to clean your clothes, cook your meals, clean up after you. We had to do a lot of housework. We have a very big house and no maid or cleaning lady or anything. It was put on to my brother and I and my father to handle all the work. He used to go down on Sunday mornings and take down all the clothes and wash them, and my smallest brother used to vacuum. I used to sweep the floor and then give it a wash. As time went on it's gone right down hill. I don't do anything anymore. I clean my own room. We don't really clean as we should. He cooks a lot and I cook a lot. It's sort of a problem. It isn't like you could come home and expect a meal on the table." At Jim's house, they have things worked out on a schedule and that helps: "I do the dishes, housework and laundry. It's part of my duty to the family. I do the shopping but Dad gives me the money."

Most people feel good about helping out at home, as Sally does: "We have a schedule and all do a lot more. That's good. Before we moved we didn't have to do anything." Duncan says: "I have more responsibility for cleaning up, making my bed and cooking. You miss it a bit, not being as good a cook as your mom, but still, you've got to learn some time. It's good experience." But not everyone agrees that the family members can get together and make things run smoothly. Laurie would help, but she feels she gets no encouragement or appreciation from her mother: "It's really weird. My father was the type that made us do everything every weekend. My mother never really cared. None of us would actually do anything around the house. Once the separation and divorce — really, nobody did anything. Once things started settling down, everybody tried to do a little bit more. It was still very disorganized. I kind of blame my mother first. Why, she isn't making everyone help. She had never really had much power over us — she didn't take an interest."

Four of the people in the group felt used by the parent at home. Sharon felt that the more she did the more she was expected to do. Likewise, at times Margaret felt like saying to her mother, " 'Hey, parents are supposed to look after kids, not the other way around.' I had to learn to say 'No'." Barbara feels she's dumped on at times because she's the girl in the family: "Before the separation we all helped around the house. Now I seem to do it all. Mom has the attitude that I'm a girl so I should do more. When she says 'more' she means everything. That is one of the most important things. I felt it was my parents' fault that I had to do all this work. When Dad was there it seemed that everything was evenly shared out. But after, it was as if the boys went their own way. They went to work and played football or hockey Saturday while Mom and I were doing the house-cleaning." But Harold feels he got more to do while the girls sat idle: "I used to help around the house. But I had to do everything and the girls did nothing, so now I've stopped doing anything unless I get something for it, like the car. I've become much more demanding for money."

Not many people really enjoy doing the housework. I guess it's part of living together, and after a divorce it's important that the remaining family members live together as harmoniously as possible. If you feel you're doing too much or carrying all the load, you will want to talk this over. It seems to help to have a schedule of jobs. Then everybody knows what his or her responsibility is and you are less likely to feel dumped on.

Most people in mid-adolescent years — around 14-16 — tend to have groups of friends as well as close friends. So the fact that most of the adolescents I spoke with said they have more friends now than before their parents' separation may just be a result of growing older. But Duncan implies that there's more to it than just normal development: "I see more of friends because they come over to my house where there's more freedom, but I like to go to their homes too, because their parents take care of you when you get to know them."

Ted feels his social life has improved as he becomes more comfortable with having friends come to the house: "I kept my friends away before because I was scared of anyone who knows me seeing my dad drunk. It was embarrassment. Now I can have friends over more openly." Abby also used to shy away from having friends over: "I didn't used to invite friends over because I didn't want them to see my parents fight, but now I do. But I have less time to go out because of my responsibility for my sister."

Some feel they have less time to be with their friends now because they have become involved in more activities. I have noted previously how joining new activities, sports or creative pursuits seemed to help some of the adolescents to keep their distancing from the pain of the separation. Elizabeth speaks very highly of getting involved in outside activities: "I've taken courses, like junior modelling, singing lessons at school, guitar lessons and dancing. It's just that extra bit that helps you through life. I think everybody, whether your parents are divorced or not, should indulge in a hobby. Now I've taken up guitar. Anything to keep me busy. What I don't have money for I'll do without — you can always go to the park with a friend. I find little ways to enjoy life. I've expensive tastes but I can do without. I'm glad I'm me. I wouldn't want to be anyone else. Over this separation and divorce I have become a more outgoing person and more understanding of individuals." Richard points out how you may need to get yourself going in this direction. Your parents may not have the energy to be concerned with your social life: "I do a lot of sports now. Before my father used to register me, but now I push myself.

My brother has just sort of dropped everything and he's getting flabby."

Having covered the major changes that the group spoke of, there are still some losses and gains I have not mentioned. I asked the group, "What do you think you lost as a result of your parents' separation?" Here are some of the answers:

Richard: "I have virtually no family life at all. I have lost it all because my father left. I tend to make my own rules and run myself. I'm not sure how to compensate for the loss of my father now that I realize how much I've missed him, except that I am seeing him a lot more and he is helping me a bit. But besides seeing him I guess I tend to make closer friends. I miss so many family things. I don't go out on Christmas. It's funny how people who have it don't notice it. You've got freedom. I'd trade it any time."

Karen: "I lost the family thing. I just miss family companionship. My boyfriend, he has a large family and to me it means a lot. It's the smallest thing but it puts so much joy in yourself. I just miss that love from being a part of the family."

Marion: "I've lost a lot — no kidding myself there — I miss my dad as a person. I miss the family and I miss the touch of class he added to the house, and I think there's a lot of hurt that I wouldn't want to go through again, but, at the same time, I've learned a lot. I hope I won't make the same mistake as my dad. You lose a lot. You don't even miss it until one day you realize it's not there."

Duncan: "I've lost the assurance of knowing my mother's always there. The guys down the street, 17 and 18, always have their mother to cook dinner and feed them. Usually my dad cooks, but if he doesn't we have to do our own. I'm a pretty good chef, you know. I don't get waited on by my mother."

Margaret: "I lost respect for my mother — and affection for my mother. I'm an exceedingly affectionate person. I don't demand it but when I get it I can take and give. I can't give and take affection with my father now. It was a security thing. If I take affection from my father now I feel guilty."

Bob: "Day-to-day dinnertime adult conversation with my father — I find in our household the only time everybody sees each other is at dinner. My mother caters to my younger brother and sister. I've taken to listening to CBC radio. I've got no one to talk to — the group of us had a greater sense of adult rapport — now I feel like a satellite."

What are the gains?

Joel: "My life has been changing in all sorts of different directions. I'm getting into film and I've some talent."

Jill: "I've stopped biting my nails. I've lost weight. I don't chew my hair anymore and my pimples have gone. I'm much happier."

Bob: "Greater knowledge about parents — certain

amount of strength having gone through something and survived it all — feel stronger than a lot of kids whose parents are still married."

Laurie: "Sometimes I think that people that go through divorce are lucky. I know you go through the hassles but you learn so much you can cope with people and life in general."

ADVICE ON CHANGES:

For adolescents
1 Don't abuse your parents' lack of rules and discipline. Make reasonable curfews and rules for yourself.
2 Find out about family finances and how you can help. A job can be good in itself.
3 Get into outside activities.
4 Is your home a place you can bring your friends? If not, talk to the family members about how you can work together to make it one.

For parents
1 Your teenagers need the reassurance and security of discipline now more than ever.
2 If you have financial problems, trust your adolescents and share your concerns. They will try to help out if they understand the need.

12
Love and Marriage.

It seems natural that a person who has seen their parents go through a divorce should be somewhat cautious about getting married themselves. On the other hand, having lived through a divorce might give one the assurance that such difficulties could be avoided in one's own marriage. Which of these assumptions is correct? I wasn't sure, so I asked some of the adolescents, "Do you think your parents' divorce has affected your own future plans for marriage?"

Jeff's answer to me was very similar to what most people said: "You know, it affects you for the rest of your life. Because my parents are divorced, marriage thoughts for myself have been put back about ten years. Before my parents split I might have been thinking of getting married maybe at 25, but right now I have no intentions until 35, and hopefully I will know the person well and I plan to live with them for a few years — in the same way as marriage. You know, with the same way except for a legal piece of paper saying two people are actually joined into one. And living together would give you a good idea of what the other person was like. It would just be the same relationship as marriage. In that way, after you've lived with somebody for a few years you could decide to marry them because by that point you would know what they were like or else you could just say, 'Well, I don't think this is going to work out and you could just leave it at that without going through so many hassles and legal papers which really make a mess out of it.''

What I understand Jeff to be saying is that although he hasn't been discouraged about the possibility of getting married, he would want to be very sure of the relationship before he became formally or legally married. Many people I spoke with agreed they'd be much more cautious about such a permanent step as marriage. They plan to wait longer before they marry than they might have. Annette says, "I'll obviously wait a long time, to be sure."

Although a large number of the young people I talked to thought it was a good idea to live together for two or three years before marriage, not everyone agreed. Some were strongly opposed to pre-marital sex. Margaret was one who felt this way: "I don't think I'll get married, at least for a while. I see what divorce can do to a person. I don't want it to happen to me. I guess, I'm kind of — you know — but I don't believe in having sex before you're married. I'm a virgin. I think that's right for me. But I plan to get married." Others didn't think that their parents' divorce had changed their attitude at all. They felt positively about their own abilities to make a successful marriage. In talking with Duncan, I mentioned that some psychologists had found that adults who were getting divorced were more likely to have parents who had divorced. I asked Duncan if he felt this might happen in his case: "I don't think so. I feel that I have whatever it takes to make it work out. I'm not worried because theirs didn't work out, but if I get married I'll stay together." Likewise, Ted feels that he can make his marriage work out because he will not enter into it too easily: "You know a lot of cases where people marry for one reason or another. I don't think I will ever be in that situation. If I ever get married I will marry the person mainly because I love them and for that specific reason only. That's what I think marriage is based on. You look at marriages these days: they're breaking up left and right, mainly because there wasn't really a love there in a lot of cases. People just feel, 'What the heck, get married. He or she has a lot of money.' That really bothers me because they're thinking of themselves and not of who they're hurting — children."

Ted has brought up the question of staying together to avoid hurting the children. Did he think that the parents' staying together might also harm the children if they had to live with a lot of fighting? He answered, "If there is true love between parents they'll get together again. But if there has been a problem — a major problem where they've been fooling themselves, depriving their children of their rights, I think divorce is the only way. It's not the greatest thing, but the only alternative. I think today people in their 20's have a better trust between the two of them. Both have to work, especially early in a marriage. They have to support each other. Hopefully, before separation there are alternatives — counsellors, priests, friends — just to talk it out. Two people should be brought together to express their feelings. You really have to love someone to tell them their faults and know it's really hurting but in the long run it can help more than it can hurt. Separation is an alternative. Hopefully, I'll never get to that point."

You may find that you don't agree with Duncan and Ted: it's natural to want to avoid what is painful. You may be saying, "I'll never expose myself to the kind of pain and hurt I see my parents going through." Elizabeth recalls how her early romantic ideas of marriage were shattered: "In the background there are fears. Ever since I was five I wanted to get married. My father was always saying, 'You'll find out.' I want to live with a guy. It has put a kind of fear in the back of my mind — I want a career but I also want to settle down. If I get married I will do everything possible to make it forever."

With time, perhaps a year or two, you may find yourself thinking optimistically, especially if you come to have a close relationship with someone. Of the adolescents in the group only one person, Laurie, was living with someone. But several people had steady girlfriends or boyfriends. Bob says this helped him: "Actually I was more pessimistic about relationships before I met my girlfriend. Now I can see a permanent relationship."

The group was much more divided on the issue of staying together and making it work or getting a divorce if it wasn't going well. Sally says that, if things were bad enough, "I'd be prepared to get divorced, but I have background in it so I know what to expect and how to deal with it." Richard is convinced he would be able to work towards a good marriage: "If my marriage was bad I'd change it — not get out." Michael agrees: "I would make more effort to communicate — it wouldn't happen to me like my parents." It appears that people are more concerned about choosing the right partner the first time than keeping the marriage together.

What about having children? Four out of five in the group wanted to have children. Two felt they would not have children because óf over-population. Jill, an only child herself, had never wanted children. But both Gordon and Barbara are worried about having children because they fear the repercussions if their marriage should break up. Barbara says, "I worry very much. My second oldest brother is separated. They have a little boy and the emotional thing he is going through — he's not talking yet and he's nearly two. He could be slow, but babysitters and his mother's boyfriend and all — it tears me up. I've babysat a lot. My mother belongs to One Parent Families and I babysat her friends. I've stayed up until two in the morning talking to teenagers who are just as mixed up as I was a few years ago. I'm really scared — I don't want that. I want to make sure if I get married it's sure to last. Staying married is very important to me. I want children. It's my goal. It's what I've been put on earth for."

At this point you may be thinking to yourself that talking about marriage and children is getting pretty far into the future. You are probably much more concerned about your own dating or lack of it than your future marriage plans. One of the sad things about being an adolescent whose parents divorce is that you are deprived of first-hand knowledge of an adult sexual relationship. I don't mean just in the bedroom. I mean the normal daily intimacies that occur between two happily married adults. I mean seeing your father put his arm around your mother while watching television, catching your mother flirting with your dad, a special look or a shared memory that makes them both smile. So, how are you to know how to behave in a close relationship? How much teasing is alright? How much flirting?

Many of the people I spoke with felt that their parents' divorce had had a major effect on their development into sexually mature men or women. The kinds of difficulties that people told me about depended on their sex and whether they were living with their mother or their father. Obviously, it might be more difficult for a boy to go to his mother with questions about sex or dating. Michael says: "If you're a boy, you feel more comfortable going to a father about dating. That's when I felt the need for my father. I can remember blaming my mother for the fact that she made me feel some pressure when I expressed an interest in going to see my father. But she got upset when I said I would like to see him when I felt like establishing a good father-son relationship. I found the answers through friends and my middle sister."

Since many of the people I spoke with talked about having an "Oedipus complex" or a "reverse Oedipus complex", I guess this type of language has come into fairly common use. I think people used these terms to refer to a situation in which a boy is living with his mother or a girl is living with her father and the relationship changes from a parent-child one to a closer, more friend-to-friend type. Each person may come to depend more on the other because of the separation. When there are two parents in the home they are more likely to discuss intimate matters with their partner. When a parent is alone, he or she may come to talk to a child in this way. If this happens, you may feel very uncomfortable or even a bit frightened.

You may react by spending more time away from home. Jim feels that his growing interest in girls helped him through a difficult time. It may be, however, that he was somewhat over-involved, as he says: "After the separation I started getting seriously involved in women, girls. I started caring more about them. It's funny — girls can just change your whole lifestyle. Like, you forget about your own family. I don't know whether it's anything to do with the divorce, but it was always me and all the other guys whose parents were divorced. We used to go out to parties with the girls. Those guys whose parents weren't divorced would have to go home at 8:00 or 9:00 and stuff like that. We'd stay out until 10:00 or 11:00. We'd go to the parties and meet all these good-looking girls. We had more freedom and more fun too. I can't speak for all the boys, but I had more fun since my parents have been divorced."

You may recall that Gordon's mother left home and moved away. He has only visited her twice in four or five years, as she lives in the West. He feels not having a mother to relate to has really affected his sexual development: "The problem for me today, I'll have to be honest, is female friends. Some of the girls that I know — I think it's a kind of Oedipal complex which sort of ties up my feelings. Girls seems almost a symbol for a mother or something. I feel inferior. I sort of look for their approval. When I was in class the other day, this economics teacher, she's been teaching for years, she made a joke. She said, 'What you need is a mommy.' I felt ridiculous because I don't believe it, but I'm sure I missed out on something. It's changing and I'm getting more confidence in myself and more self-assertive."

You might suppose that a girl living with her mother has it easier. But Jill says she started dating earlier because of her parents' separation: "As soon as they got divorced I went out with a much older guy. I was 13, he was 17 or 18, 'cause I suppose a father substitute — but also to get away from Mother to take me out. But that got out of my system. I rushed into it earlier than I normally would." Elizabeth began seeing many boys but, like Jill, felt this was a substitute for an affectionate relationship with her father and a reaction to what she thought, at first, was his not caring for her: "Before the separation I didn't know anything about sex. I really wasn't interested. After, I went out a lot. I got to know guys a lot. I didn't know the dangers when I was 12-13. I needed a lot of male companionship — I missed my father. I missed the father-daughter relationship, whereas when I was 9 or 10 I didn't really need him as much as my mother. At 13 I used to turn to male companions, taxi-drivers, my brother's friends, just to talk to. We had nothing going, as the saying goes, but I just wanted a friend to talk to. Before then I was an introvert. When I was 14 I looked about 17 and that was a problem. Some girls might say, 'Hey, wow! You're lucky,' but since I wasn't I had trouble with guys thinking I was older than I really was. I had to have the police around the house a couple of times because they were annoying me. I was hauled down an alleyway, which was frightening. I've never told my father. Guys today don't bother me. I'm 17 and they're my friends. I treat them as a normal human being. Since I had trouble with males when I was 14 I have gotten to know different types of males. One will just take your body, if I can say that. The other type takes you as a person. I had to be aware of this, being on my own, not being around my father. I would go out on the town with my friends. I got in with the wrong gang: they liked smoking and drinking and picking up guys. I had a friend about a year and a half after I got into this gang, she dragged me out of this gang. Also, now I have a boyfriend who has helped me a lot. He just sits there and I just talk to him. It's the greatest companionship. I once talked for about an hour and a half to him and he didn't say anything: he just sat there and understood everything I was saying. Now if I had to relive this all I would change some things." Elizabeth seems to have worked her difficulties out well. If you find yourself getting into this kind of dating pattern, you might want to take time out to sort out what's happening to you. Perhaps, if Elizabeth had visited her father more often and had a chance to talk to him about everyday happenings, she would have felt less need to constantly seek male companionship.

Margaret's reaction to her father's absence was exactly opposite to Elizabeth's. Rather than looking for substitutes, she avoided boyfriends: "Yes, it hindered my sexual development. I'm a virgin at 18. I'm the only person I know, but it doesn't totally relate to my parents' situation: I just haven't had a relationship with a male. I was Daddy's little girl — now he's gone. I find that hard to deal with."

Barbara is also somewhat hesitant about getting too close to anyone: "My relations with boys — I'm shy, I'm quiet. I have to get to know them and feel very comfortable before I can act myself. I don't know exactly why, but I think the divorce has something to do with it. Maybe the fear of getting emotionally involved."

Sometimes a parent who is concerned about his or her child may foster the idea that it can be dangerous to get too close. Laurie's mother, having experienced the pain of a marriage break-up, wanted to protect her from the same pain. Laurie feels she was also bitter towards men in general: "Yes, I was always brought up that sex was a sin unless you're married and when my parents were divorced it was always shoved down my throat — 'You see what I mean. You just don't have sex unless you're married.' — and it put a big block in my head, and when David and I first started to have sexual relations it was very hard. I couldn't enjoy it. It just kept running through my head — the divorce. 'If we break up, am I wrong in doing what I'm doing? I want to do it and if this is what I want it can't be wrong,' and then I kept thinking back on what my parents have said. It was a pretty rough time. The divorce changed my situation more than my ideas. I figured if you're not sleeping with every man in the city, if there's one special man, it's okay. I used to live out of the city and my boyfriend came 50 miles every weekend to see me. That was okay. But in spring break he wanted me to come to visit him and meet his family. Well, automatically I was committing a sin. 'What will people think? You're a little tramp running all over the country.' " Laurie talked to her friends and they saw no harm in it. But, "My mother caused a lot of problems between this guy and myself. My mother is very bitter about her divorce. It seems all this ties in with the divorce. Ever since she's got no one, no person is worth having. Once David and I had an argument. My mum says, 'Where's David?' I said, 'Oh, he's not talking to me right now.' She says, 'Just like your father.' She says things like, 'Don't put money away in the bank; he'll up and run away with it,' and 'All men are the same.' It's funny but it's caused some problems between David and me. His family is divorced too. We're both afraid of marriage. I've been living with him for eight months now. We've talked a lot about divorce. I keep thinking I know I love him but I don't want either one of us to go through what our families did."

The effect that your parents' dating can have on your own dating has been discussed elsewhere, but special mention should be made of how upsetting it can be if your parents' dates are also interested in you. Although it is unusual for such a relationship to go very far, what happened to Abby and her mother's boyfriend may be a warning to avoid such situations: "With Mom having a boyfriend it was scary. I didn't know what to do. I'd get really mad and he'd say nothing was going to happen and it was awful. He'd make passes at me. I think I might look at men more negatively now. If people remind me of him I just stay away from them."

I think Abby could have told her mother what was happening, but if she feared her mother might feel competitive and angry then she could tell an adult family friend. It is probably wise not to tell the other parent except as a last resort. You can imagine the kind of difficulties and accusations that would occur if a father thought his daughter was being bothered by her mother's boyfriend.

All people who are 11-18 years of age have to handle the normal problems of developing sexually, and having parents who get divorced during this time of growth may cause some problems. Some in the group, however, felt that their sexual development wasn't affected in any way. They felt it led to earlier maturity and a more realistic approach. Bob says, "As of last November, I've been, I guess what you might term 'going steady' with, well, a girl I've been going to school with now for, you know, the last thirteen years and what I've found, well, what I attribute to the separation and divorce of my parents is that I sort of — all the sort of romantic 'I'll love you forever' sort of thing has, you know, has completely passed me by. I just can't think that way anymore because I've got a feeling that there's nothing permanent about love at all and I guess I'm a little bit cynical about love although I think it's probably, you know, the only — a very important road to happiness. On the other hand, the separation has given me a chance to do an awful lot of discussing with both my parents and my friends, and perhaps the attitude I've adopted is more realistic than the sort of fairy tale look towards love. My girlfriend's parents are married and she has the same sort of attitude. Maybe it's just the effect I have had on her. I don't want to make it sound like a negative one because I think it's been a very positive one. She feels the same way about that sort of thing."

I think that the fact that so many of the adolescents in the group had good feelings about having a boyfriend or a girlfriend is significant. Many of them also knew people — of either sex — who were just good friends. These friends were often supportive and helpful.

ADVICE ON DATING:

For adolescents
1   Do date if you want to.
2   Dating should not be your only out-of-home activity. Take a second look at other possibilities.
3   Keep in contact with both parents. Write your father or mother if you haven't seen him or her in a while and need to talk to him or her now. The worst they can say is, 'No'.
4   Be cautious about accepting advice which starts with "All men are... "or "All women are... "

For parents

1   Try to help your adolescent cope with the emotions involved in love — sexual information is not sufficient.

2   Regulate your child's dating frequency even though he or she will fight you on it.

3   Retain your place as the parent, a mature adult in whom your children can confide. Don't reverse the roles.

13
We Still Fight Over the Television.

Do younger brothers and sisters have it harder when it comes to separation? It seems that they do. Really young children may have trouble comprehending what's happening. Annette found that her little brother had trouble understanding: "One hard thing was that my brother was only five years old at the time. He didn't understand exactly what was happening so I had to explain to him because he was scared to go to my mom or my dad. So I told him what was going on. He still didn't understand. It's just lately he's beginning to understand. He has to face the fact that my dad's remarried and he has kids." Younger children have difficulty accepting the permanence of the separation even when parents remarry. They keep hoping that their parents will get back together. Elizabeth said, "It didn't bother me but it bothered my young sister. She was hoping they'd get back together. She picked sides. My sister was too young to see there were no sides."

You may find yourself having to try to explain what's happening to your younger brother or sister.

Jeff recalls how important he was to his little brother. It was very difficult for Jeff when he had to leave him and move away with his mother: "My brother was 10 years old. He took it very hard. With a boy that young it is a hard thing to take. His problem was that he couldn't really understand why; why his parents would split up after they'd been together for so long and for what reasons. It was just a little too hard for him to comprehend. I had to take the job as sort of like the leader over the three kids in the family. I'm younger than my sister but I would say that I could handle things a little better than she could — my brother also. He looked up to me and we try and discuss things together. We would always stick as a group."

Dawn agrees that in her experience young children can be more disturbed by the absence of one parent: "My sister is 14 and my brother is 8. My brother was probably the most upset because my brother and my father were very close. My brother really enjoyed the time we had with my father when we went out with him." Sometimes brothers or sisters who are between the ages of 8-11 may seem much more hurt and angry. They may appear to have more difficulty in handling this anger than you do. Jim found that both his older and younger brothers had more problems handling their feelings than he did: "My younger brother was more upset than my older brother and me. He had always had a lot of friends, but he turned into a recluse. My older brother — I didn't know if it had anything to do with the divorce — but he started getting into crime. He was drinking and taking drugs. A change started to come over him. He changed for the worse. He quit school and got kicked out of the house. Then my younger brother started getting into trouble. I guess it was just the friends he hung around with."

But brothers and sisters are able to offer each other
a great deal of support and understanding. Many of the
adolescents I spoke with said that they are now much
closer to their sisters and brothers. Sally said, "We all
became much closer, especially my younger brothers
and I. When my father was there none of us were really
close. When my brother started to look at me as his
older sister to whom he could turn for advice, it was
really great. The first time he wanted to take a girl out
he asked me what to do. It's funny — it made me feel
really good." Similarly, Barry found that he could
share dating problems as well as talk about mutual
family concerns with his sister: "After the divorce I
was just so close to my mother and sister. I guess you
have to be to survive. All of us work together for
something we want, like a car. That makes the unity
much stronger in our family. We can also share losses.
If my sister or I break up with a girlfriend or boyfriend
we can share it and talk about it and it's good. I gained
respect for my sister. I realized they are human beings.
I talk a lot more with them, especially about divorce
and separation."

It's sad when this closeness is broken by the family
dividing and brothers and sisters splitting up. Sometimes this break makes it almost impossible to get back
the same sense of closeness. Laurie was able to help her
younger brother but eventually it meant her moving
out and providing a home for him herself: "One of my
brothers went with my father. He was the only one. He
was the brother who introduced this woman to my
father. My mother wanted nothing to do with him. But
when he wanted to come home I was really excited. My
mother talked to her friends and they thought he had
changed and realized what he'd done wrong. She said,
'Okay he can come home but he's going to have to

pay rent and he's going to have to do his fair share around here.' Well, now since he came home it's been sheer hell for him. I wish he would leave. My mother treats him like a dog. He got busted on a dope rap last year and that seems to give her the excuse — he's disgraced her name. But since it didn't hit the papers he can go on living at home. He had to live in a cold, damp room in the basement. I came to the city about 8 months ago and am living with my boyfriend. We brought my brother to live with us as well."

Sometimes, a split occurs between brothers and sisters even though they continue to live in the same house. This can happen when people start taking sides. As Jerry put it, "All the relatives line up. The split doesn't stop with the parents. Brothers and sisters are torn apart." Bob explains how this happened to him: "My brother and sister slightly took the side of my mother and I slightly took the side of my father. This is most noticeable when we have family discussions. If I am in an argument or discussion with my mother, my sister and brother sort of come running to her assistance and tell me to stop it, saying, 'Leave Mom alone.' My mother seems to cater more to my brother and sister, and they don't like talking about things that I consider important."

How can you prevent this from happening? You can probably best help your younger brother or sister by allowing them to gain a gradual understanding of both your parents. While you appreciate your little sister's or brother's loyalty to one parent over the other, you know that in time he or she will come to understand how complicated a separation can be and that it isn't a black and white situation. At first Barbara found herself somewhat alienated from her brothers by her concern for her father and her anger at her mother for, as she saw it, "kicking him out." Since this affection for her father was reciprocated by her dad, she began to suspect that her brothers were jealous. But she had trouble making sense of all the facts. She describes how her brothers helped her see both sides: "I wondered, sometimes, why my dad didn't love my four brothers as much as me. He never said he loved the boys like he did with me. But I guess, being older, they had seen more drinking. Later there were lots of fights between my older brothers and myself. All the relatives, like my grandparents, blamed me for keeping my parents together for so long. Then it started to get better with my brothers. They told Mother to help me when I was really angry and confused. They became very protective and caring. They have been really kind and considerate. I get along perfectly well with them now." Sally found her older brother to be just as tolerant: "My brother is older. He helped me see things I didn't understand. Before, we fought a lot — it wasn't good. Now we've had to help each other."

Of course, it's only natural for brothers and sisters to continue to have normal family squabbles. Bill, who is the youngest of three boys, says, "Since the divorce my brothers haven't bullied me as much, but we still have problems with control of the T.V. channels." Whether you become closer to your brothers or sisters — as most people I talked with did — or find yourself with opposing views, you will probably note a change in the way you are with them. Sally summarizes it this way: "My brother and I are closer now. I think it can't remain the same. Either you get closer or you get farther away."

During the early weeks of a separation, and often for

some time after, parents are not able to cope on their own the way they once did. One parent may have difficulty organizing the household chores while another may find shopping and planning too much. When this happens, an adolescent member of the family may have to step in and help out with some of the household responsibilities. Usually, extra help around the house is gratefully accepted. But what do you do if an older brother or sister starts acting like a parent and telling you how to behave? Laurie said this happened to her: "My oldest brother felt he had to be the boss of the house. I didn't like that at all. We have never been close. He said if we didn't do what he wanted he'd beat us up. He always thought I was a little kid, too. I was a girl, not a boy. He'd ask my dates when they were bringing me home — he was worse than my mother." When he went away to university Laurie felt relieved.

I wonder if there isn't some other solution. Perhaps there is a way of diplomatically letting an older brother or sister know that you appreciate their help but not their interference. Bob's family let him know when they thought he was taking on too much responsibility: "As the eldest I carry more responsibility. The other two are more observers, while I'm more of an adult. Right afterward I was acting like a father, but my mother didn't like it and my sister didn't like it."

It might help to remember that this adult role is not one which everyone takes on willingly. Margaret found herself stepping in out of necessity: "After divorce I became a substitute parent for my younger brother. It was not my wish but I became more like a friendly advisor. My mother won't parent so I have to." Annette appreciates what it is like both to be bossed around and to feel responsible for her younger brother: "Sometimes my older brother tries to act like he owns the house. We fight like brother and sister. But with my younger brother he needs discipline, so I help to give him more discipline."

Rather than act as a parent an older adolescent may be called on to run interference for the younger children in the family. As the older, Elizabeth explains that she sometimes has to protect her sister, while at other times her sister is very supportive of her: "My sister, I always considered her as a mouse and me as a cat. She would hide in a hole and I would be a little too big for the mousehole to get in and I would be the one who was slapped around. My sister was under my mother's protection. I felt I was the 'black sheep'. However, my sister was my best friend. It would have been very difficult without my sister's help. Although she's 2 or 3 years younger than I am, she comes in helpful. In times when you're lonely, we go see a movie or just out to a park, especially when my mother wanted to be alone. It got to a point where I was looking after my sister and I felt like a mother to her. My mother did very little in bringing us up — my mother would go away and leave a neighbor in charge, but I was the real babysitter. If Father ever found out he would be really mad."

Having to take charge, or being given heavy responsibility, can be very difficult, especially if you feel that your younger brother or sister is not doing his or her part. Karen feels that her younger sister is not pulling her load: "I get along very well with my sister although many times I have to act like a mother to her and be responsible when my mother is away. She's expected to do some chores but mostly it's up to me. I've accepted responsibility and my sister hasn't. She

202 My Parents are Divorced, too

tends not to work that much in school and not to do
what she's told. I have to be home after four to look
after her.''

It takes time to develop mutual respect. The
closeness that some of the people I spoke with
described came gradually. They had to work with their
brothers and sisters on sharing responsibilities. Ted's
efforts and those of his brothers have paid off in their
becoming closer and more caring of each other. He
says, "I guess I take on more responsibility, being the
oldest. It's a mixture between wanting to and a need.
I'm the oldest living with my mother but my brothers
took on a parenting role. I'm much closer to them
now — there are not barriers.''

ADVICE ON HELPING BROTHERS AND SISTERS:

1 Share with your brothers and sisters not just the
   chores but your concerns as well.
2 If you're living apart, try to see each other frequently.
3 Help younger brothers and sisters understand both
   sides. If they're angry, help them talk it out.

14
Final Words.

Looking back over the last few years, what would you most want to tell someone whose parents are getting a divorce? These final words of advice from all members of the group are the products of their own unique experiences. Obviously, not all the advice will be useful for any one person. You must decide what is the best course of action for you. These words of advice speak for themselves with sincerity and perceptiveness about the distress you might experience.

Abby: "It's hard at first because you're going through changes in all your relationships, but later on it will stabilize. I'm glad to share my feelings with other people. I hope it will help you. I know I would have wanted something like this to help me understand all the feelings I had. I felt totally lost and alone.

"I would say to try to stay mutual between them (your parents) and to try to keep your own identity for what you feel instead of feeling badly for other people and feel what they'd think and what they'd like to hear. Stay neutral and give support to both parents. Assume more responsibilities than you had before — it really helped me. I've seen a psychiatrist before and that's really helped to talk about it. If somebody else told you to talk to your mom and she says bad things about your dad and vice versa, it's good to have someone outside.

"Realize your feelings are normal. Try to help out the parent you're living with."

Barbara: "Don't be too hard on your parents or yourself. Don't be so sensitive and don't let yourself be sensitive, because you'll just get hurt. I don't mean to wall yourself off totally — that wouldn't be good either."

Margaret: "Be strong. Hold your head up and don't think you're anything less than you are. Keep as many people around you as possible, for security for one thing. Just sort of live your way through it from day to day.

"Don't alter your thoughts about other people as a result of it. I guess that's it. Just keep yourself in one piece and think as much of yourself as you ever did.

"It wasn't so hard as I thought it would be: everybody lives through it. I know my father better. Everybody goes through traumas and everybody survives. At the beginning, I thought I wouldn't get through."

Laurie: "I remember going through the divorce. I said, 'Sure lots of people get a divorce, but I bet you I'm the only one.' Well, I was positive nobody had it as bad as I did and I imagine everybody thinks that.

"Parents have it just as hard as kids. It's harder bringing up kids by themselves. They don't have each other to talk to. For example, parents might talk it over and say, 'Hey, watch this guy. He's not right for you.' One parent has to make decisions by herself. I wish I'd never walked all over my mother — we were very selfish and never took time out to think. Try to look at it from both sides, both self and parent."

Michael: "If your parents are divorced and you've got to live with one of them but you still feel an attachment and a need for the other one, but you feel pressure from the parent you're living with about going to visit the other one, then you kind of have to understand the parent — how they might feel threatened. But I don't think you should abandon it. I think you should make an effort to see the other one, because you need both parents sometimes."

Jeff: "Don't get caught in the middle. Live where you want to live. Visit when you want to go. I hope my words benefit you. I wouldn't want anyone else going through such a bad scene."

Harold: "All I can say is that if you know your parents are separating don't exploit one and forget the other because the one you forget will forget you and that's the hardest pill to swallow.

"Marriage should be worked at. Marriage should be thought over before entered into. It can be a good thing, but a lot of hurt can come out of it which can be avoided."

Gordon: "Find out what's happening as it affects you. Insist on explanations. Ask if they still care.

"In some cases, if a separation doesn't occur parents can't grow as individuals. They can't move on. I'm happy that it was so peaceful and I didn't have to worry about the problems that would have resulted if they'd stayed together. In the long run it helps. It's an experience — I'm a survivor. Whatever does not kill me strengthens me."

Annette: "Talk to your best friend. Talk to someone. Don't worry — there's not much you can do. Don't be all depressed 'cause you'll just make your parents feel worse and they feel bad enough as it is."

Sally: "Give positive opinions. Don't listen to negative stuff, like putdowns. If no one in your family will do this then go to a counsellor.

"Everyone has to realize the feelings of everyone who's involved. That's hard."

Bev: "It's hard to accept, to get over it. Talk to your parents about it. It's different for every kid.

"Parents should realize it's as hard for kids as for them. Kids never really accept that parents didn't get along. Let kids know if they're having problems; not fight in front of kids, but don't pretend things are great. Better to find out from parents beforehand."

Joel: "Try to keep out of the situation. Try to be neutral. It's a difficult task. Sometimes it can be easy: it can be just a signature on paper. But sometimes, and most times, you get something that causes it to be difficult. Mine was, but look at me — I've lived through it and it's just one problem that took not a day but five years. I've lived through it. Everyone has difficulties and problems in life. Just have love and understanding for your parents and don't pick sides."

Jerry: "It's basic survival. It's funny. I've always lived with my father. Once it's started you can't stop it. Find out more about the legal stuff, sometimes you don't know what you're getting into."

Jill: "Keep in touch with your feelings as well as your parents' feelings."

Ted: "You know what's going on just living in the city. You see it around. Keep cool — observe. Help both sides when possible, but don't take sides.

"As far as I'm concerned, ten-year-old people should be taught in schools — no matter what kind of school — the problems affiliated with alcohol."

Richard: "It happens. You've got to learn to live with it."

Jim: "Not to worry. Let it happen — it's natural. Things will work out for the better — and if they don't work for the better you'll just adjust to it."

Duncan: "See your parents often. It's hard not having the love of a mother and the daily care of a mother and all that."

John: "Hopefully, eventually you come to know it's better, a positive thing, once everything is sorted out."

Barry: "Look for a release for your anxiety and bad feeling. It's up to you to decide what it is."

Bill: "Try to visit as much as you can. It's great if you live close enough so you can drop over after school. Parents should try to see kids as much as they can."

Bob: "Talk to your parents and try to get both sides of the story."

Marion: "Be as objective as you can. Help yourself by keeping yourself separate."

Elizabeth: "At first I thought no one loved me, but I've learnt that my father loves me as much as my mother, even though my mother sees more of me. So you see, separation and divorce of your parents isn't the end of the world. You've got to live through it. It was difficult and I never thought I would make it, but I think now I can see the rainbow at the end of the road and it's all settling down. Sure, in the future I'm going to come across other problems to do with my mother and father. They couldn't be half as bad as what I've gone through. We worked it out. As they say, 'Life must go on.' Just keep busy and have love and understanding for your parents and don't pick sides because there are no sides. No one is right and no one is wrong. Everyone has their own views. I don't wish for some other life or some other home."